P9-DEW-002

The Insider's Guide to Winning Education Grants

The Insider's Guide to Winning Education Grants

Dakota Pawlicki

Chase James

Foreword by Gregory Michie

JOSSEY-BASS™
A Wiley Brand

Cover design by Michael Cook

Cover image by © MDI Digital/Getty

Published by Jossey-Bass
A Wiley Brand
One Montgomery Street, Suite 1200, San Francisco, CA 94104–4594—www.josseybass.com

Jossey-Bass books and products are available through most bookstores. To contact Jossey-Bass directly call
our Customer Care Department within the U.S. at 800-956-7739, outside the U.S. at 317-572-3986, or
fax 317-572-4002.

Permission is given for individual classroom teachers to reproduce the pages and illustrations for classroom
use. Reproduction of these materials for an entire school system is strictly forbidden.

Wiley also publishes its books in a variety of electronic formats and by print-on-demand. Some material
included with standard print versions of this book may not be included in e-books or in print-on-demand. If
the version of this book that you purchased references media such as CD or DVD that was not included in your
purchase, you may download this material at http://booksupport.wiley.com. For more information about
Wiley products, visit www.wiley.com.

Library of Congress Cataloging-in-Publication Data has been applied for.

ISBN: 978-1-118-41290-9 (paperback); ISBN: 978-1-118-59292-2 (ebook); ISBN: 978-1-118-59513-8 (ebook)

Printed in the United States of America

FIRST EDITION

PB Printing   10 9 8 7 6 5 4 3 2 1

Contents

Acknowledgments   ix

The Authors   xi

About UNITE   xiii

Foreword   xv
Gregory Michie

Introduction   xvii

First Period: Grants 101   1

Second Period: Composition   19

Third Period: Creative Writing   37

Fourth Period: Economics   67

Fifth Period: Personal Finance   93

Sixth Period: Statistics   107

Seventh Period: Communication   127

Appendix A: Templates and Worksheets   139
    Project or Program Planning Template   139
    Proficient Example: Needs Statement   141
    Example of a Likert Survey Template   143
    Practice Worksheet: Word Count I   144
    Practice Worksheet: Word Count II   146
    Practice Worksheet: Needs Statement   148
    Practice Worksheet: Budget Categories: Fourth Period   149

Practice Worksheet: Ledger Activity: Fifth Period   151

Answer Worksheet: Word Counts I and II   153

Answer Worksheet: Needs Statement   155

Answer Worksheet: Budget Categories: Fourth Period   157

Answer Worksheet: Ledger Activity: Fifth Period   159

Appendix B: Resources   **161**

Comprehensive Chapter Review Guide   161

Exit Ticket Answers   165

Fifty Classroom and School Grants   167

Flowchart: The Grant-Writing Process   170

Grant-Reviewing Committee: Proposal Evaluation Rubric   171

Request for Proposal: Health Awareness Evaluation Rubric   171

Complete Proposal: Instructional Unit   173

Example of a Classroom Instructional Unit Grant   182

Example of a Teacher Travel Grant   186

Example of a Final Report of a Grant-Supported Program   194

Index   **197**

For UNITE members across the nation and the students they teach

Acknowledgments

URBAN NEEDS IN TEACHER EDUCATION (UNITE) is a dynamic nonprofit organization whose membership consists of talented and dedicated pre- and in-service teachers around the United States of America. These educators self-select to continue their professional development on their own time to better teach the students in their classrooms and serve the urban communities in which their schools are situated. This book is a result of the persistent fervor in which UNITE teachers demonstrate in the pursuit of new knowledge and skills. It is our hope as authors that we capture the spirit of UNITE and bring the knowledge of our organization and its members to a wider audience.

Although UNITE is thankful to the many individuals who have seen to its success over the years, we would like to especially thank those by name who have made this book a reality:

Colleen Burger: editor

Kathryn Kloepper: contributor of materials and book design

Greg Michie: friend, advisor, and forwarder of material

Kari Podany: contributor of materials and visual images

Kim Heilenbach: contributor of materials and book design

Joseph Roth: book design

Gregory Fairbank: book design

Eva Lawrence: book design

This book is made useful by its many exemplars, interactive tutorials, and online content for which we relied heavily on practicing teachers and philanthropic organizations to provide a wide array of coverage across contents and grade levels. These insightful works were provided in part by Carmela Balice, the Chicago Foundation for Education, Donorschoose.org, John Dudley, Katie Lyons, Megan McCoy, Michael Mettenburg, and Rachel Perveiler.

Finally, thank you to the friends, family, and supporters who have made UNITE, this book, and so much more a reality. Without your constant presence, our work would cease to matter.

The Authors

DAKOTA PAWLICKI is president of UNITE (Urban Needs In Teacher Education). The lead author and presenter for UNITE's grant-writing teacher professional development series, Dakota is coauthor of a multimillion-dollar federal Teacher Quality Partnership grant received in 2009. After teaching in Chicago Public Schools, Dakota joined the Chicago Teacher Education Pipeline at Illinois State University, where he currently serves as operations manager, developing and coordinating teacher-preparation programs.

CHASE JAMES, executive director of UNITE, has experience writing and editing grant proposals ranging from small classroom projects to multimillion-dollar programs for schools and nonprofit organizations. In addition to his role at UNITE, Chase is an educator in the Chicago Public Schools, teaching social studies at Collins Academy High School in the city's North Lawndale neighborhood.

About UNITE

UNITE (URBAN NEEDS IN TEACHER EDUCATION) is a nonprofit organization aiming to enhance the preparation of teachers in our nation's most underprivileged and underrepresented schools. Since its founding in 2006, UNITE has grown from a small, on-campus group at Illinois State University to a national nonprofit serving thousands of educators annually. UNITE provides professional development for preservice and in-service teachers on topics ranging from classroom management and grant writing to special education and gangs. UNITE works actively with schools, universities, and colleges of education across the nation.

To learn more about the organization or to schedule a UNITE grant-writing workshop at your school or district, visit www.urbanneeds.org.

UNITE

Foreword

During my first year as a teacher in Chicago, the resources available to me were confined to a tall metal cabinet in a corner of my classroom. The best thing that can be said about that cabinet is that it was full. But the praise ends there. Its shelves were crammed with dusty dittos, outdated textbooks, faded worksheets, and reading passages that bore little relevance to the lives and experiences of my students.

I remember opening the double doors of that cabinet many times and just staring inside, hoping something different—something I could actually use to help teach my students—would magically appear. It never happened.

I pieced together a curriculum the best I could that year, but the lack of resources was a constant challenge. Our school's budget was tighter than tight, and I had almost no knowledge at the time of what assistance—financial or otherwise—might be available beyond my school's doors.

Over two decades later, teachers in Chicago and many other school districts across the United States still face dwindling budgets and limited resources. Underfunding of K–12 education combined with expenditures focused on high-stakes testing have meant cuts to arts programs, after-school activities, and even basic classroom supplies. In the summer of 2013, protestors converged on the Chicago Board of Education to draw attention to a new round of funding reductions. One teacher held a sign that read:

Dear students,

Due to recent budget cuts, please bring the following supplies on the first day of classes:

toilet paper	hand soap	teachers
paper towels	books	teachers' aides
markers	pencils	nurse
one case copy paper	floor wax	

Sometimes as a teacher you have to laugh to keep from crying. But you also have to take action. In part, that means raising your voice in the struggle for educational equity—protesting, blogging, joining with grassroots teacher activist groups. But it also means arming yourself with the know-how to sustain your classroom and provide for your students when you don't have adequate resources.

That's where this book can help.

Dakota Pawlicki, Chase James, and the other young educators who contributed to *The Insider's Guide to Winning Education Grants* understand the process of grant writing inside and out. They've done it for their own classrooms. They've helped others do it. They've led workshops and created helpful resources for teachers. And now all of their knowledge and experience are collected in this incredibly useful book.

As the authors point out, what you'll learn in these pages was probably not on the radar screen of your teacher preparation program. You may have learned a lot about curriculum construction, alternative assessment, or technology integration, but through it all, the unspoken assumption was likely that you'd have the resources you need once you landed in a classroom of your own. Far too often, that's not the case.

I've known Dakota, Chase, and many of this book's contributors since they were undergraduates studying to become teachers. What impressed me about them then, and what continues to now, is not only their unwavering commitment to working with students in under-resourced schools but also their determination to bring other teachers along for the ride. These young educators are not satisfied with simply closing their classroom doors and doing the best they can for their twenty-five or thirty kids. Like all good teachers, they want to share what they've learned with colleagues. They want to effect change on a larger scale, and this book is just one fruit of their labors.

So, don't just stand there staring into a cabinet full of decades-old textbooks or pointless worksheets like I did my first year. Close the cabinet doors, gather some colleagues together, read this book, and start writing that first grant.

GREGORY MICHIE
AUTHOR, *HOLLER IF YOU HEAR ME:*
THE EDUCATION OF A TEACHER AND HIS STUDENTS
CHICAGO, ILLINOIS
AUGUST 2013

Introduction

It is no surprise that schools are cash strapped. We see it each summer as states and districts get ready for the upcoming year. What programs are being cut this year? How many teachers do we have to lay off? How big will my class size be? States with broken budgets are unable to pay promised dollars to school districts, and with per-pupil spending increasing each year, lawmakers at all levels are having to make tough choices to balance budgets.

Traditional teacher preparation does not prepare teachers for these conditions. In fact, it doesn't even prepare teachers for these conversations. Teachers leave their program ready to get kids to learn, work with parents, and collaborate with a team of like-minded educators. Most teacher-preparation programs do not include coursework in business, budgeting, or education policy. Some in our nation believe that teacher training should not even include training on how to teach . . . that a degree in something combined with a couple of weeks of training on managing a classroom qualifies to teach in the United States' toughest schools.

Educators not equipped with the knowledge and skills to keep their schools fiscally afloat are at a disadvantage. This book is for those teachers who want to take action. As teachers, we cannot wait for others to straighten up our financial house. We must aggressively pursue opportunities for self-growth and learn the very game that poses the greatest threat to education: the game of money. This book is much more than simply a how-to guide for writing and winning grants. It is a survival book for teachers and districts everywhere. This book, and the process it outlines within its pages, is a lifeline to those who seek to bring stability to their classrooms (not to mention supplies, equipment, and opportunities).

We hope you find it useful. We hope you find it insightful. Most of all, we hope you join us in bettering our profession and taking control of our schools once more.

How to Use This Book

The pages that follow provide a step-by-step walk-through on writing education grants. The process, strategies, and suggestions offered are best practices assembled by the authors from many practicing educators with a proven success in writing grants. Whether you are writing your first classroom grant for less than $500 or are part of a seasoned grant-writing team gearing up for a multimillion-dollar grant, this book has something for you.

Tip 1. If you have never written a grant before, we suggest reading the book in its entirety *while* writing a grant. UNITE, the nonprofit organization sponsoring this book, offers a classroom grant each year. Sample RFPs (request for proposals) can be found in appendix B. After each chapter, complete the respective portion of the RFP incorporating the techniques discussed. At the end of the book, you will have a complete grant proposal ready to be submitted to UNITE and could potentially win your very first grant!

Tip 2. Dig out those old grants and have them handy. Perhaps you have won some and lost some over the years and you are reading this book to hone your skills. Take out your old grants and review them while reading through these chapters. There are many examples taken from winning grants right here in this book. Take a moment to compare the voice, presentation, and format of these winners against your own.

Tip 3. Jump around. Although this book can be read as a whole, it can also be used as a reference text. If you are having trouble with budgets or need to get some fresh ideas on incorporating data into your projects, jump to those chapters for a quick refresher.

Tip 4. Interact with the book. There are many interactive features within the book that are aimed at improving your skills as a grant writer. Make sure to use them completely. Also, check out the appendixes for resources and examples that can be used in your next proposal.

Tip 5. Follow Grant as he ventures through the book with you. Grant will often have useful insights, reminders, tip, and tricks that you may want to note as you work through the pages.

Tip 6. Realize the full potential of this book. Although the main focus of this book is writing excellent education grants, there are many other pieces of advice that go well beyond the grant-writing and -winning process and into turning your school into a resource-producing machine. The authors and contributors have a diverse background as educators and nonprofit professionals. By combining their knowledge of and skills in the classroom with the unique expertise of running a nonprofit, they have created a resource that blends techniques on finding and securing new money while maintaining good relationships with donors.

This book is meant to be used by teachers, administrators, preservice teachers, universities, counselors, and other school personnel. By reading this book, the reader will be equipped with the knowledge on how to write small classroom-based grants as well as large grants that can be used to fund whole programs.

Not a teacher? The advice, strategies, forms, and other tools included in this book can be used by parents, students, administrators, school board members, and anyone else interested in winning education grants.

Many education professionals find themselves limited when writing grants. Most teachers and administrators will apply for grants for technology or equipment because that is usually the first thing to get cut from budgets. We want to encourage you to think beyond the immediate needs of the classroom and consider writing larger grants for your school. Some ideas that you may want to consider while reading this book are as follows:

- Start or support service learning and civic engagement activities.
- Start small learning communities.
- Create after-school opportunities for youth.
- Develop partnerships with local organizations, other schools, universities, or other entities to achieve a project.
- Hire staff to run a special program.

Ideas are endless but by thinking a bit bigger, you may find and realize more opportunities than you had previously thought possible.

Congratulations on taking the next step to reach your professional goals, and good luck!

> To download many of the templates and worksheets from this book, go to www.wiley.com/go/educationgrants

The Insider's
Guide to Winning
Education Grants

First Period: Grants 101

You are a first-year teacher. You have elaborate dreams of immersing your students into a rich, hands-on curriculum on a daily basis in order to enhance their learning experiences. You yearn to travel with your students through new, exciting worlds and push them to thinking beyond anyone's greatest expectations. Your dreams are limitless, until you awaken and realize that you are teaching in a school that has not allocated funds for extracurricular activities, resources, or curriculum enhancement. You realize that you cannot begin to pay for all of the expenses that come along with enriching activities, especially on your teacher salary. You start to think of your students and how hard it will be to explain to them that you simply have no means of gathering these extra resources for their learning . . .

Whether you are a first-year teacher or a twenty-year veteran, this situation may very well apply to you. Luckily, through the power of grant writing, you can overcome these obstacles. We are excited that you have decided to join us as we break down the complex and frightening world of grant writing into teacher-friendly examples and strategies. We hope after reading this book and putting it into practice, the only conversation you will need to have with your students is, "What project should we complete next!?"

Throughout this first chapter, you will develop an understanding of grant-writing basics—why grants exist, where to find them, what types are available for educators, and how to write them using key vocabulary. We will end this chapter with an analysis of a common RFP (request for proposal) and ask you to start searching for some grant applications that interest you.

Each section in this chapter (and each chapter in this book) is a key component to turning your dreams into realities for your students. Grant writing can seem like an overwhelming endeavor, but with the right set of tools and tricks, you will be well equipped to provide your students with a well-rounded, exciting education that is bursting with a variety of new experiences with all expenses paid!

"Show Me the Money"

Whenever we hear people talk about grants, the scene from *Jerry McGuire* comes to mind, when Tom Cruise and Cuba Gooding Jr. yell, "Show me the money!" (If you haven't seen the movie, search "Show me the money" on YouTube.) Many people think of receiving a grant as winning the lottery or getting that big signing bonus for entering the education profession (wouldn't that have been nice!). Show me that free money! To an extent, they are correct. Grants are "free" money, but that money comes with guidelines, reports, deadlines, and results.

A grant is a monetary award that is used to establish, implement, or sustain a project or program.

Grant writing is almost a misnomer. You don't actually write a grant. You write a proposal and hope to win a grant. You receive a monetary award to use in order to establish, implement, or sustain a project or program; that monetary award is known as a grant. Grants come in all shapes and sizes, but they all have one thing in common—you have to work hard to win them.

Grants exist for a variety and usually a combination of reasons. Many organizations center their mission on supporting people or other organizations that do good deeds. Offering a grant is one way that organizations can provide support to others and fulfill their own mission at the same time. Grants also offer the convenience of claiming a tax-deductible donation on annual tax reports for the funding organization. This is why grants are usually awarded only to charitable entities—501(c)3 organizations and schools.

Types of Grants

This book focuses on education and classroom grants under $5,000, although we will mention strategies that you can use if you are applying for a larger grant. Although grants range from small monetary awards to large monetary awards (we have seen grant opportunities for $50 and some for $5 million) and can cover a wide range of possible programming in a variety of professional fields, all grants fit into one of three distinct categories: rolling deadline, revolving deadline, and one-time awards.

Rolling deadline. If a grant is classified as *rolling*, the organization accepts proposals at any time. Think of it like a rolling college admissions process. The college accepts applications as they come until all spots have been filled. The granting organization will accept proposals until the allotted funds are all allocated. Usually with a rolling deadline, the funder will specify that applications will be reviewed during certain intervals throughout the year (monthly, quarterly, semiannually), and awards are given after reach review session. The American Honda Foundation offers education grants on a rolling deadline basis:

Deadline for submission	Anticipated board review	Anticipated grants awarded
February 1	April	May 1
May 1	July	August 1
August 1	October	November 1
November 1	January	February 1

The American Honda Foundation grants are rolling grants because there are multiple times of the year that you can submit a proposal (February, May, August, and November). Each interval has its own timeline for review and awards. If you submitted a proposal to the American Honda Foundation on August 10, your proposal would fall into the November–January–February time frame, because you missed the August 1 deadline.

Revolving deadline. Grants that have a set application window that becomes available every year are known as *revolving* deadlines. The UNITE Classroom Grant, similar to many small education grants, is a revolving grant because the RFP is announced annually on March 1 and proposals are accepted only through the end of March. The annual application window changes from grant to grant but will usually stay the same for a particular organization. The Dollar General Literacy Foundation offers a summer reading grant that becomes available every January and has a specific deadline for its application window. Once the application period is over, you will have to wait until the following year to apply.

One-time award. As the name implies, this type of grant is offered only once. A one-time award will have an application window, just like the revolving grant, but once the deadline is passed, the grant will no longer be available. You have a one-time chance to apply and receive funding. Many state and federal grants are one-time awards. These types of grants also have the tendency to have a larger monetary value and want to see a program implemented over a longer time frame, between one and five years. One-time grants usually will also have a more lengthy application process and will require a team of experienced writers and reviewers.

Grants Are Right Around the Corner

Seriously, grants are all around you. The trick is learning how to search for them and then keeping an up-to-date list of available grants that meet your eligibility requirements and align to your school's needs.

Many different organizations offer grants, and each organization has its own philanthropic goals and objectives. It is important to understand who offers grants in order to find them and write a successful proposal catered to the funding organization. We have taken a moment to describe some of the common entities that offer education grants.

Foundations. Foundations are organizations that are established to give out money. Most foundations are 501(c)3 organizations. Check out the mission statement of almost any foundation, and it will say something along the lines of "supporting," "addressing," "developing," or "investing in" certain initiatives and programs. The most common way for a foundation to support, develop, or invest in is to offer monetary awards—grants. There are several types of foundations. The type and focus area of the foundation will determine your ability to receive funds based on your project or program. Common types of foundations are listed in the following paragraphs.

Family foundations. Established by a family or individual in remembrance of his or her family, family foundations can range in size and available funds. One of the most common family foundations is the Bill and Melinda Gates Foundation, which awards millions of dollars a year to a wide range of programs, including education. The application process for a grant from the Bill and Melinda Gates Foundation is highly competitive, so unless you have a team of experienced and proven grant writers, it may be best to keep this foundation as a bookmark in your Internet browser for now.

There are hundreds of smaller family foundations across the country, and many of them support local education initiatives that have a less-competitive grant-application process. Take, for example, the Zeist Foundation in Atlanta, Georgia. This family foundation offers monetary awards to education initiatives in its local region. Here is the mission statement of the foundation taken from its website:

> The Zeist Foundation embraces a holistic approach to address
> the needs of at risk children, youth and families in the areas of
> education, arts & culture and health & human services. The
> Foundation seeks opportunities to leverage its investments in
> organizations that are innovative, collaborative, and sustainable
> in serving children, youth, and families.

Notice the use of the terms *address* and *investments* in its mission statement. This organization offers multiple education grants each year to fulfill its mission. Family foundations like the Zeist Foundation are present in cities across the nation.

Private foundations. Private foundations share many characteristics with family foundations. These types of foundations are a little less common but still can be found in metropolitan and rural areas across the country. An example of a private foundation based in Denver, Colorado, is the Piton Foundation, which focuses its philanthropic goals and funding on programs that operate within a forty-square-mile area of land on the outskirts of Denver called "the Children's Corridor." Many private foundations have specific guidelines for funding within a specific geographical area. If there is a private foundation in your area, reach out to leaders of the foundation as soon as possible. It can be a great resource for your school.

Corporate foundations. Large companies like Walmart and Lowe's will create a separate branch of the company under the foundation model. Corporate foundations are funded through the profits of the sponsoring corporation or the corporation's owners and board of directors. Similar to other foundations, each corporate foundation will have its specific goals and focus when distributing funds. Most grants offered by large corporate foundations will ask how the proposal intends to use volunteers from the corporation or affect employees and families serviced by the corporation. The Walmart Foundation actually gives out three different types of grants: local, state, and national. It is important to read the guidelines in each grant application to determine which level of funding you should apply for when considering large corporation grants. Much like the Bill and Melinda Gates Foundation, the national level of large corporation grants can be very competitive.

Local community foundations. If you are lucky, you will find a small local community foundation that has a very specific giving mission. These foundations are similar to small family foundations or private foundations but are not operated by a family or individual. Usually local community foundations are funded through multiple individual trustees, supportive organizations, and business donors. The Chicago Foundation for Education is a local community foundation that offers education grants only to teachers in Chicago public schools. The Chicago Foundation for Education supports on average more than one thousand Chicago public school teachers each year! A great place to search for local community foundations in your area is at your local house of governance, school district headquarters, and city website.

Other 501(c)3 organizations. Other nonprofit organizations that hold 501(c)3 status also award education grants to teachers and schools. UNITE falls into this category, because we are a 501(c)3 organization but not set up as a foundation. Many similar education nonprofit organizations will offer monetary support for teachers.

Donor's Choose, a popular teacher grantlike website also falls under this category because it is a recognized 501(c)3 organization. Donor's Choose provides a venue for teachers to post projects and receive donations to fund their proposal. Donor's Choice will be mentioned a few more times throughout this book. Although different from traditional grants, many of the writing tips and project assessment guidelines in this book will also apply to Donor's Choice grants.

Business support. Another source of funding that is often overlooked is various business grants offered in your community. Many businesses, small or large, have allocated funds for community giving. Some large businesses that do not create a foundation branch, such as Target, offer grants directly from the business side of the company. Reach out to community-based businesses in your area and ask if the business offers any type of monetary (or volunteer) support for teachers or schools. You will be surprised how many will say yes!

Government. Some of the largest providers of grant funding are government organizations. These are organizations situated within the local, regional, state, or national government. Oftentimes, these grants are tied to legislation and can either be competitive or noncompetitive. Typically, government grants allow schools and broad-based partnerships to complete large-scale work in efforts to meet an objective or new set of standards established by officials.

There are many places to begin looking for government grants (your local elected official's office for one), but a good place to start is with the United States Department of Education (DOE). The DOE offers many useful tools that can shed light on federally funded projects that could benefit your school. The US DOE maintains a useful education resource organizations directory at http://wdcrobcolp01.ed.gov/programs/erod where you can search for resources that align with your desired project or school priorities.

Now that you have a general understanding of the types of grants and who offers them, the next step is to find grants that apply to your classroom or school! This is a common question we hear during our grant-writing workshops: "Where do I actually find the grant application?"

Well, you are in luck, because we have taken care of a lot of the legwork for you! In appendix B, we have compiled a list of fifty grants available for classroom teachers and school districts. This is by no means an exhaustive list. This list includes grants that we thought would be a great place to get started. You will not be eligible to apply for each grant we have listed in this book, but we encourage you to start sorting through the grants used as examples in the chapters of the book (like the several we have already mentioned in this chapter) and those listed in appendix B and start creating a spreadsheet of grants that interest you. Make sure you include if the grant is rolling, revolving, or a one-time award on your spreadsheet. In the future, this will help you prioritize and schedule your time working on applications.

In addition to this book, there are quite a few other places to start searching for grants. Researching the local organizations and foundations in your community is a great way to become familiar with smaller grants available in your area. When searching online for foundations, organizations, and businesses that award grants, be very specific in your online search engine. Don't just type in *grants*. You will get a million irrelevant website links. Instead try searching, for example, *grants awarded Lancaster county Nebraska*. A targeted search like this will provide links to periodicals publicizing grants that have been recently awarded. Read through these articles and take note of grants that were awarded and who awarded them. A specific search like this will also bring up foundations and organizations that have received or award grants. Try a search based on your school's geographic area, following these guidelines:

- Use a combination of key words such as *grant, award, school*, or *classroom grant*.
- Target a specific area—city, county, state.
- Search for foundations in your local area (example: *foundation Tulsa, Oklahoma*).

General searches are not a bad idea every once in a while. For example, type in *classroom teacher grant* into any search engine and see what happens.

We also recommend checking out the Foundation Center's website (www.foundationcenter.org). This website offers a great search engine tool for finding foundations offering grants across the nation. It also features articles and updates about major grants awarded, grant applications currently available, and research and reference sources. The Foundation Center Online also offers a membership subscription service for an annual fee. Signing up for this feature will unlock a multitude of extra search features throughout the site, but unless you are a school district official who is committed to writing multiple medium and large grants each year, you probably will be fine just using the free services.

The Foundation Center also offers a free newsletter service called the *Philanthropy News Digest (PND)*. This newsletter will send you regular e-mails with national news and available grant applications. The *PND* webpage also

Don't forget about using your phone. Although the Internet is quickly becoming the communication and research tool of choice, a good old phone call to local businesses, foundations, or city council's office can still provide you with some important information and help you establish a personal relationship with the staff members of potential funders.

offers an "RFP of the day." No matter what your level of commitment to writing grants may be, we recommend signing up for this free newsletter by going to www.foundationcenter.org/pnd.

Staying abreast on grants is also as easy as setting up Twitter and Facebook accounts. Yes, that is right, "tweeting" and "liking" can actually help you find grants! Both the Foundation Center (@fdncenter) and *Philanthropy News Digest* (@pndblog) have Twitter accounts and post updates on grant applications and regional and national awards. Many organizations and foundations also have Twitter and Facebook accounts. When researching foundations in your community or region, check to see if the foundation uses a social media venue and use it to your advantage. Not only will you stay up-to-date on grants offered, but you can also gain knowledge about the organization as a whole, which can be used to strengthen your future proposal!

> Follow UNITE on Twitter (@urbanneeds) and Facebook (www.facebook.com/urbanneeds) for updates on other small classroom grants released for teachers.

Learning the Lingo

Before you begin writing, it is important to have a general understanding of some key terminology used in most grant applications. The terms listed here are fairly common words you will find in most grant applications regardless of the size or type of the grant.

RFP (request for proposal). The official announcement from an organization or government entity to apply for funds. The RFP will contain all the guidelines and requirements for eligibility, funding, and submission. Most RFPs will contain the actual grant application sections and questions for you to complete, and others are just the public announcement of the grant opportunity.

Grant application. The actual form or format that you need to complete or follow to submit your grant proposal.

> Note: *RFP* and *grant application* will be used interchangeably throughout the book.

Proposal. The completed application in response to the RFP. Each RFP will specify the contents and format of the proposal. (The proposal is what you will be writing. You don't actually "write a grant"; you write a proposal to receive a grant.)

LOI (letter of intent or letter of inquiry). The initial letter to a grant funder that is required to be approved before you actually apply for funds. The LOI shows your interest and sincere intent to apply for funding if given approval. Most small classroom grants under $5,000 will not ask for an LOI.

501(c)(3) organization. IRS status identifying a nonprofit organization as tax exempt. These organizations are also known as charitable organizations. All public and private schools are designated 501(c)(3) entities. Some for-profit schools have a different designation.

EIN (employee identification number). Specific number issued by the IRS used to identify organizations, companies, and schools. Ask your school administration or school clerk for your school's EIN if needed on the grant application.

Program officer. The contact person from the funding organization who will address questions or concerns during the application and submission process. If a program officer is not identified in the RFP, you can call the funding organization's main office and ask to speak to whoever is in charge of the grant or community-giving department.

> Throughout the book, we will introduce more terminology that is common in many grant applications. The terms already given are the initial vocabulary you need to know as you begin to analyze an RFP.

Analyzing the RFP and Grant Application

Before we start discussing the actual writing process, we want to take some time for you to become familiar with certain sections of RFPs and grant applications. In the following are some of the common sections you will find in an RFP and grant application. Remember, most of the time the grant application is included within the RFP. Not all of these sections will be in every RFP that you find.

Summary of funding organization. A brief synopsis of the granting organization usually will be present. This summary gives you some important information or history of the organization, its mission and vision, and possibly its philanthropic focus or goals. Although this summary will give you a basis for learning about the organization, you will still need to complete some more in-depth research on your own. This will prove helpful as you begin writing. For example, in chapters 2 and 3 we mention using some of the granting organization's own word choice in your needs statement and goals and objectives.

Description or purpose of grant program. This section will give you information on the actual purpose of this particular grant. The funding organization will describe the award and provide an overview of the focus of the grant. Some RFPs you come across will have a very broad purpose of the program. Others will be more focused, such as this example from the Humane Society's Education Mini-Grant:

> The purpose of the Mini-Grant is to provide funds for classroom teachers who lead innovative, standards-based programs and curricula in humane education, specifically the teaching of kindness and respect for animals and their natural habitats.

In this example, the purpose is clear—to provide funds to educators who teach humane education. Although most schools don't have a humane education course, teachers can use their own subject matter to teach a unit or project about animals' natural habitats or endangered species. This section of the grant will assist you in determining your eligibility to apply for this grant and in developing your project to meet the RFP's focus.

Award amount. This section will be short and sweet, telling you how much money will be awarded. Some RFPs will offer multiple awards totaling up to a certain amount, and others will select only one proposal to fund. Make sure in your proposal not to request over the maximum amount specified.

Specific rules or policies. Each RFP will have a list of specific rules that must be followed. These policies will vary from one RFP to the next, but most of the guidelines will be fairly straightforward. Make sure to adhere to each rule or policy listed. Failure to do so could result in your application being disqualified or promised funding withdrawn. The following show two examples of rules set forth in the Humane Society's Education Mini-Grant:

- Funded projects must be the applicants' original creation. The Mini-Grant does not fund the purchase of pre-packaged lesson plans or curriculums. The purchase of office machines and computers is not funded. It will, however, fund the purchase of written materials, technology, or software to be used in the project.

- No part of this grant may be used, directly or indirectly, to influence legislation at any level of government, either through efforts to influence legislators themselves, or through efforts to influence the views of the general public on legislative matters.

Make sure you do not just gloss over the RFP rules and policies. Reading and following them will ensure that all your hard work writing a proposal is not in vain.

Proposer eligibility. This section explains the eligibility requirements for the grant writer. After finding an RFP and reading the grant description, you should check out this section next. Read the proposer eligibility section very carefully to make sure that you are in fact eligible to apply for the grant. Certain RFPs will be available only to teachers or schools in a certain state, county, or even city. Sometimes eligibility will also depend on the size, type, and demographics of your school or district. If you are not eligible, don't apply. There is no wiggle room on the posted eligibility requirements for an RFP.

Would your school be eligible to apply for the Lois Lenski Covey Foundation (LLCF) Library Grant Program, based on the following eligibility requirements?

The LLCF library grant program provides grants to libraries for the purchase of books for children preschool through grade 8 [Early Reader books through Young Adult and Hi-Lo books]. We will consider applications for school libraries and for bookmobile programs, as well as for non-traditional libraries. Non-traditional libraries are those within or operated by charitable organizations [501(c)(3)] or other non-taxable entities that have lending libraries where young people may check out books to read or to use for gathering information. Examples of such organizations include youth or family resource centers, detention centers, organizations serving young people with mental or physical health challenges, etc. In this latter category the Foundation will consider purchasing books to be used by young people preschool through grade 12, but as with other libraries only Early Reader through Young Adult and Hi-Lo books may be purchased. Only libraries or organizations within the United States, its territories, or commonwealths are eligible.

Timeline. Each RFP will specify the application window and deadline date. Some RFPs will also note the timeline after the submission deadline, including dates when winners will be notified, money will be distributed, and deadlines for final reports and completion of the program. As with previous sections, make sure you follow the stated timeline and do not miss deadlines.

Here is an example timeline section from the Lois Lenski Covey Foundation (LLCF) Library Grant Program:

We have one grant cycle per year:
- Applications for library grants typically become available on this website on or around February 15th.

- The due date for sending the completed application is June 15th. This is the last date that an application should be postmarked. Do not waste money sending an application via express delivery.
- We send grant notification and checks to award recipients by December 15th. The list of recipients will be posted on the "News" page of this website by December 21st.

Submission process. Most organizations are moving to an online submission process, but there are a few that still use the traditional type-and-mail procedure. The RFP will give you details about the submission process. Pay close attention to any information about cover letters, additional permissions, and formatting. If you are required to type up your proposal and mail, fax, or e-mail it to the funding organization, you will need to follow any and all formatting guidelines. The formatting guidelines may appear under the submission process section, application guidelines section, or both.

Sometimes you will come across foundations or organizations that publicize their philanthropy and lists all the grants they have awarded, but you won't find an RFP or grant application anywhere on their website. Some foundations accept proposals only from organizations or schools that they invite to apply; this is called a closed or invite-only submission process. Don't just shrug off a foundation that has a closed submission process; send them information about your school or classroom and try to set up a meeting with the director or program manager. Realize that getting on the invite list may take some time, but in the end, it will be worth it!

The Zeist Foundation mentioned previously in this chapter has an invite-only submission process:

Grant applications are accepted through an invitation only process. At the request of either a foundation staff or a board member, an organization may submit an on-line letter of inquiry through Foundation Source, our web-based application platform.

Contact information. This provides you with the contact information of the organization and the name and contact information of the acting program officer to address any questions that may arise during the application and submission process.

Proposal evaluation criteria or rubric. Only a handful of RFPs will actually contain information about how the reviewing committee will evaluate or score the submitted proposals. If this information is included, use it to your advantage. Much like a rubric you may give to your students, this evaluation criteria will give you a great framework to plan and write your proposal. To see an example of a grant proposal rubric, check out appendix B.

Application. The actual grant application will be a series of questions, ranging from the proposer's contact information to your program's budget. The typical application sections are described in further detail throughout this book.

We have included a mock RFP in the following. Read each section of this RFP and decide which of the previously mentioned sections is being featured. Then, write it on the lines provided.

> Not all RFPs have every one of the sections we discussed. Some RFPs will combine sections or leave out sections altogether.

> After you finish this book, you can view completed proposals that were submitted based on this RFP in appendix B.

EXAMPLE

Request for Proposal: Health Awareness Classroom Grant

SECTION 1:

The mission of our organization is to support classroom teachers across the nation who are promoting projects that increase students' mental and physical health awareness. Our organization believes that mentally strong and physically healthy students will achieve high academic standards and succeed in postsecondary education.

_____

SECTION 2:

Our organization believes that one of the most effective ways to affect student learning is to fund grants that allow classroom teachers to develop healthy lifestyle units and projects. Each school year, our organization awards grants of up to $500 to worthy projects that significantly influence student learning and promote mental and physical health awareness.

_____

SECTION 3:

Our organization will accept grant applications from July 1 through August 15. The grant process is competitive in nature. A committee composed of outside experts in the field of health education will review all qualified grant applications and make recommendations on funding. A maximum of five awards will be given.

The Health Awareness Classroom Grant program promotes health education activities in classrooms from kindergarten through twelfth grade. The program encourages development of innovative health awareness activities within the prescribed curriculum. Only full-time classroom teachers in a public or private accredited elementary, middle, or high school in the United States are eligible to apply.

Your application may be revised and edited until the final submission deadline at 11:59 PM EST on August 15. Winners will be notified by October 1.

SECTION 4:

All requests for funding must conform to the grant guidelines and submission instructions in order to be considered. Failure to complete any of the required information will result in the rejection of the proposal.

- Grant proposals are judged on a competitive basis and may not be funded or only partially funded.

- Funds must be used on the proposed items. Funds must be used within six months of approval or the funds will revert back to our organization.

- The Health Awareness Classroom Grant program promotes health education activities in classrooms from kindergarten through twelfth grade.

- Grant recipients should include our organization in any publicity regarding their grant.

- Grant recipients will be expected to announce their grant to the parents of students participating, school faculty, and in a school publication.

- Teachers are encouraged to send pictures of the project in use by the students as well as copies of any publicity involving the project and related activities.

- One grant per teacher, maximum of two teachers per school, will be considered under this program.

- Identical grants cannot be submitted multiple times by multiple individuals in the same awards year.

- Previously awarded grants will not be eligible for funding for the next funding cycle. They may be resubmitted every two years.

- Grants must be submitted under the name of the teacher who is leading the project.

Funds will not be considered for the following:

- Registration fees for competitions
- Tee shirts, promotional items, or awards

- Teacher workshop fees
- Activities that benefit fewer than twenty students

SECTION 5:

All proposals must be received via our online submission portal found on our website.

An end-of-project report must be submitted no later than six months from the date the grant is awarded. Grant fund expenditures are the responsibility of the grant winner, and an itemized list of expenditures must be included in the final grant report. If not received within the time period, the applicant will be ineligible for future grants until a report is submitted and received by our organization. No applications will be accepted after August 15, 11:59 PM EST.

Our organization will announce the winners no later than October 1.

SECTION 6:

Please type responses to these questions in the online submission form located on our website. No attachments will be allowed.

1. *Needs assessment:* State why the funds are needed for your particular classroom. (maximum of 300 words)

2. *Project description:* Provide a detailed description of the planned activities. How will students' overall health benefit? Include your unit or project objectives. Include a proposed timeline for the project. (maximum of 500 words)

3. *Teaching method:* Describe the teaching methods you will use to implement your project, and describe how and when you will implement your project. (maximum of 150 words)

4. *Outcomes and evaluation:* Describe the expected outcomes and evaluation methods you will use to measure your project's success. Be specific. (maximum of 300 words)

5. *Vision:* Describe your vision and plan for replicating or adapting your project within your school or district. (maximum of 150 words)

6. *Project budget list materials, equipment costs, and so on needed to implement your project:* List each item separately. Provide a total amount for all expenses.

Let's see how you did with this exercise!

Section 1: We hope this first section was pretty straightforward. This is the "summary of funding organization." It contains the mission of the granting organization and some of the goals about giving.

Section 2: This section is the "description or purpose of the grant program." Although short, this section gives the reader the basic reason for the grant and its monetary purpose. The "award amount" is also included in a brief statement within this section.

Section 3: Here the granting organization combines "timeline" and "proposer eligibility" into one section. It specifies the opening and closing of the grant application, describes those eligible to apply, and even includes some guidelines about the proposals accepted, such as who will be evaluating the proposals and the maximum number of awards that will be given. This is a great example of how no RFP will exactly follow the sections that are outlined in this chapter. Each RFP will be composed in a different format, but most RFPs will contain the same general information.

 More information about communicating with the funder and reporting the implementation of your program is highlighted in chapter 7.

Section 4: The format of this section is very common to see under a "specific rules or policies" section. A bulleted list of vital guidelines and rules will be included in most RFPs. Take particular note of the guidelines of what will not be funded by this RFP (tee shirts, registration fees, etc.). We recommend rereading this list of policies and rules before you submit your completed proposal just to make sure you don't accidently disqualify your hard work by forgetting one of the stated policies or rules.

Section 5: This short section would most likely be the "submission process." This section states how to submit your proposal, via the online submission portal, and notes that a follow-up report will be required six months after the funds are given. Also note that the deadline and award notification dates are mentioned again in this section.

Section 6: Finally, the "application" section featuring the questions that you will need to answer in your proposal. We highly recommend typing out your responses using a word processor on your computer and then copying your responses into the online form for this type of submission process. Also note that word counts are listed to guide you in the length of your responses. Word counts are explained more in the chapter 2.

Stop and Find an RFP

Before reading the next chapter, we encourage you to stop and find an RFP that you are eligible to apply for and provides funds to a project that interests you. Check out our list of classroom grants in appendix B and choose one that you can refer to as you continue reading about writing style, word choice, and each section of a grant application. Seriously, stop and find an RFP and print it out or have it minimized on your computer so you can reference it to gain more understanding about writing a proposal.

Once you have an RFP in front of you, read on and get ready to write! At the end of each class period, or chapter, we will include a quick bulleted list of highlights from the chapter called the "Review Guide." These are key takeaways that will help you quickly reflect on what you have just read. We have also included a comprehensive list of these sections from each chapter in appendix B as a quick review tool before writing a future proposal.

First-Period Review Guide

- Grants are monetary awards used to establish, implement, or sustain a project or program.
- Three categories of grants are rolling deadlines, revolving deadlines, and one-time awards.
- Grants are right around the corner! Foundations, corporations, nonprofit organizations, businesses, and the government all offer education grants.
- When searching online, use specific search criteria and focus on your geographic area. Don't forget to use social media to your advantage.
- Review the key terminology found in RFPs and grant applications.
- Each RFP is unique, but most contain similar terms and content.
- Most RFPs will contain the grant application questions or direct you to an electronic submission form.

Each chapter will conclude with a quick exit ticket to test your knowledge of the topics, terms, and skills covered in the chapter. Think of it as a quick review quiz over the material you just read. The answers for each chapter's exit ticket are also included in appendix B. Good luck!

 After each review, Grant, our proposal-writing student, needs to take an exit slip before leaving the class and turning the page. Join Grant and take the quizzes with him. He always does better when he has your sheet to look at!

First-Period Exit Ticket

1. Which of the following is not a type of grant deadline?
   a. One-time award

   b. Rolling

   c. Annual

   d. Revolving

2. *True or false:* All RFPs will contain information about how your proposal will be assessed.

3. *True or false:* Businesses cannot award grants because a business is not a recognized 501(c)3 organization.

Second Period: Composition

Finding and analyzing a grant application is only the first step in the grant-writing process. Next comes the fun part: writing! If you are like most people, your palms began to sweat simply by considering the thought of authoring a text. Before you close this book and run away, though, consider the catalyst for almost every composition. Most times, remarkable writing is born from a writer's passion. Rarely crafted on a whim, great works are often a written catharsis of a powerful moment—an injustice, an inspiring event, an unexpected encounter. As an educator, you are lucky, because you already have your passion: your students' success. Channeling this passion will propel you into great writing and, with any success, a winning grant application.

In this chapter, we will focus on strategies you can use as you begin writing each section of your grant application. Becoming an effective grant writer takes practice and critical analysis, but, from basic grammar skills to unique writing techniques, this chapter will give you a firm foundation. We recommend rereading this chapter every time you start a new grant application, because reviewing and practicing the strategies in this chapter will ensure that your passion for student success is able to shine through.

Before the Pen Hits the Paper (or Your Fingers Hit the Keyboard)

The blank page can be very intimidating. Luckily, you can stall the actual writing process a little longer while you assemble the necessary tools. Here is a quick checklist for you to reference before you pick up the pen:

- ☐ Access to the Internet
- ☐ School mission and vision statement
- ☐ School, school district, and state report cards
- ☐ Standardized assessment scores, for both your class and schoolwide
- ☐ Specific demographics of your school, district, community, and state

☐ Any credible research on your topic (articles, website links, cited quotes, etc.)

☐ Research and data from similar programs or projects that you are proposing

☐ Anecdotal evidence and student or parent surveys

☐ This book!

We recommend gathering as much of these materials as you can. If you are a paper person, print it all out, and set it in front of you. If you like everything electronically accessible, create a folder on your desktop, and keep all your research and data reports on hand in that file. Staying organized and being prepared will greatly improve your overall grant-writing experience and help you stay focused on writing a winning proposal.

Despite your best efforts, though, you undoubtedly will not have everything you need when you start writing your proposal. Along the way, you will have to do some more research, find different data or school reports, and ask your grade-level head or administrator for clarification and approval. The more grants you write, the more this process will become routine, and if you continue to write proposals for the same programs year after year, much of the research and data collection will already be done.

Putting Your Ideas into Words: Writing Style

You have found and analyzed the RFP. You are getting familiar with grant vocabulary. You have gathered some research on your program topic and collected pertinent school and district demographics and data. Now, you must develop your style. Your writing style is the most vital piece of the proposal, so we have compiled ten quick tips and strategies to help you frame and develop your voice.

Using just one or two of the strategies will not be sufficient to develop your grant-writing style. Each of the strategies is equally important and must be used in conjunction with one another. By reviewing all the strategies as a cohesive unit, you will greatly increase your chances of winning your next grant proposal.

Tip 1: Think of Your Proposal as a Conversation with Another Teacher

Think of how you would address another teacher at a conference or professional development. We hope your conversation is professional and conventional. When writing a small-classroom or school-based grant, you want to write your proposal as if you were talking to another professional colleague who shares your ambitions and expertise. The grant-reviewing panel is not an old friend from high school or your college roommate. However, the panel is also not your boss with the power to hire or fire you. They are simply colleagues who want to see you succeed, so your proposal should maintain the qualities of a professional, conventional, goal-oriented conversation.

Here are a few examples to help put this professional, conventional tone into perspective. The following describes the students featured in a grant proposal. Examine the statements and place each of them into one of these three categories:

State, federal, and non-education grants need to lean toward the professional side of the conversation. Think of a large state or federal grant as a conversation between a principal and a superintendent, instead of two teachers. Throughout the book, we will make sure to provide tips and extra strategies if you are working on one of these larger grants.

- Two casual friends out of the workplace
- An informal conversation in the teachers' lounge
- Two colleagues interacting at an educational conference

Example A: All of my students in Room 204 struggle with reading and math. I know this because of the students' standardized tests scores. The majority of my students qualify for free and reduced lunch and do not have access to the Internet or other resources at home. Our goal as a class this year is to raise both our reading and math scores by two years of growth.

Example B: All of my students in Room 204 need to improve in both reading and math. On their NWEA assessments at the beginning of the academic year, 90 percent of my students were at least two years behind in reading and three years behind in math. The majority of my students qualify for free and reduced lunch and do not have access to the Internet or other resources at home. By using the school initiative of implementing minilessons and differentiation, our goal of two academic years of growth is attainable.

Example C: All of my students are pretty slow. They struggle with basic concepts in both reading and math. The teacher last year

> totally didn't teach them what they needed to know, and they
> came to me way behind where they should be. The fact that most
> of them come from poor homes in bad neighborhoods doesn't
> help their chances. We are really going to try to improve this year,
> but it is going to be tough.

Working backward, we think you will agree that example C was an excerpt from a conversation between two casual friends in a nonwork environment (but we hope you don't talk about your students like that at school, or, for that matter, anywhere!). Example C calls the students *slow* and blames the previous teacher for the students' academic shortcomings. Using politically incorrect terminology for students' home life is a sign of unprofessionalism and not recommended when writing a grant proposal (see tip 6). The phrase "really going to try to improve" connotes that this teacher doesn't really believe in his or her students.

Examples A and B are very similar, but there are a few critical differences in the word choice. Example B is more likely to be heard between two colleagues in a professional environment because the details and word choice are more precise. Rather than just stating that students are *struggling*, based on standardized tests, example B paints a more comprehensive picture of the classroom, referencing the specific standardized assessment and providing actual data (*two years behind in reading and three years behind in math*). As you continue to read the rest of our writing style tips, you will see why this is important.

Reread the last sentence in example A and example B. If you had to place a bet on which classroom would achieve their goal, which would you choose? Although both examples have the same end goal, example B articulates a more confident action statement. When writing your proposal, you are trying to convince the funding organization that your project will succeed and achieve your stated objectives. Make sure that your word choice exemplifies your belief in your students and your proposed program.

Tip 2: First versus Third Person

If you have read any other grant-writing book or how-to guide for writing grants, you probably have been told to use the third person over the first person in most circumstances. This is true. However, classroom grants fall into one of those circumstances in which you can use the first person to your advantage. We recommend really analyzing the RFP and researching the funding organization before deciding whether to write your proposal in the first person or third person.

Here is some advice when deciding which point of view will be most beneficial for you:

First person	Third person
• The RFP asks you to specifically describe your classroom and your students.	• Your proposal describes multiple projects to meet an overarching goal for an entire school or district.
• There will be one person (you) who is responsible for implementing the classroom unit or project.	• Multiple community partners will be involved in the project.
• Your proposal describes one project specific to your classroom or your school.	• The project will not be completed in one academic year.
• The prompts in the RFP are written in the first person. *Example:* "How will you assess this project?"	• The RFP was published by a national organization or a state or national government and gives nationwide awards. *Example:* Department of Education Race to the Top grant.
• The RFP was published by a local organization or foundation that funds only local or region awards.	
• The project will be completed in less than one academic year.	• The prompts in the RFP are written in the third person. *Example:* "How will the project be assessed?"
• The RFP is for $5,000 or less.	• The RFP is over $5,000.

There are pros and cons to writing from both points of view. Describing your classroom in the first person creates a connection with the reader and shows your relationship with your students. However, the third person creates the perception that you are unbiased, because you do take ownership of the students or classroom. Check out what we mean by looking back at examples A and B under tip 1. Both are written in the first person, but in the following, we have rewritten example B in the third person. In what ways do your perceptions change as you switch from the first to the third person?

> *Example B:* The students in Room 204 need to improve in both reading and math. On their NWEA assessments at the beginning of the academic year, 90 percent of the students were at least two years behind in reading and three years behind in math. The majority of students in Room 204 qualify for free and reduced lunch and do not have access to the Internet or other resources at home. By using the school initiative of implementing minilessons and differentiation, the class goal of two academic years of growth is attainable.

Whichever point of view you choose, make sure you stick with it for the duration of the proposal. You will run into an editing nightmare if you go back and forth within the proposal.

Tip 3: Your Proposal Is Alive and Active!

When writing your proposal, always frame your work in an active voice. An active voice makes your proposal sound alive and focused because it always provides a subject for the action taking place, giving the reader the mind-set that this program *is* going to happen! There is nothing wrong with the passive voice, but keeping your proposal in the active voice will focus the audience on the future actions of your project. Take a moment to practice this skill in the following, switching the action statement from passive and then back to the active voice. A few examples have been completed to get you started.

Passive: Literary-focused minilessons will be created and implemented across all grade-level teams.

Active: Lead teachers will create literacy-focused minilessons to implement across grade-level teams.

Passive: The after-school program will be supervised by parent and community volunteers who have been recruited.

Active: The two lead teachers of the after-school program will recruit parents and community volunteers to help supervise students.

Passive: The progress of the project will be monitored by three different assessments taken by the students during the course of the year.

Active:

_____

_____

_____

_____

Passive: Monthly visits to each school will be made by the school district instructional team to evaluate the program, and feedback for improvements will be provided.

Active:

_____

_____

_____

_____

Tip 4: Leave the Slang on the Streets

This may be one of the more obvious rules, but we thought it couldn't hurt to mention it. Do not include slang terms in your proposal. Terms like *thugs* or *gang bangers* should make no appearance in a grant proposal.

An example of less obvious slang is *Audy Home,* a term used to describe a juvenile detention center or halfway home for at-risk youth. *Audy Home* does not necessarily carry a negative connotation, but it is slang that your audience may not know what it is. If you are wondering if a term is slang, then, rule of thumb is, you shouldn't use it.

Not so much an example of slang, but keep in mind words or abbreviations used in your school building that may not be commonly used across education mediums. One example in our school would be *MBC* which stands for *marker board configuration,* or each teacher's agenda and objective for the day. Make sure to explain any terms unique to your school or community in your proposal.

Tip 5: Your Project Is Not "Out of This World!"

Leave the hyperbole to your students; you stick to the facts. The project, unit, or program in your proposal will probably be run very well and have a positive impact on your students. Is it going to be "earth-shattering" or "create world peace"? No. Make sure you describe your program with facts and details, but don't make it sound too good to be true by using vague or grandiose terms and phrases. Take a glance at the following examples and write down some of the words or phrases that are clearly exaggerations not based on research, data, or facts about the program. Feel free to chuckle to yourself when a program is being described as "out of this world!"

> *Example A:* Our *Parents in School Program* is going to change the face of parent interaction with neighborhood schools! Every third Wednesday evening of the month, our school is going to hold an academic decathlon in which groups of parents and students will compete for prizes. This component of the *Parents in School Program* is going to exponentially increase student engagement at school and decrease misbehavior referrals because the atmosphere will be contagious and lead to greater support at home for each and every student.

_____

_____

_____

_____

Example B: Jackson Junior High is planning to create a one-of-a-kind student empowerment program focused on keeping at-risk students off drugs and out of gangs. After just one year of this programming, 100 percent of students at Jackson Junior High will be drug free, and no students will be involved in gangs! This program has the potential to change lives across the country!

_____

_____

_____

_____

Example C: The students at Kingsley High School want to start a Model United Nations program after school. This nationally recognized program and curriculum has posted incredible results focused on student leadership, public speaking, and college entrance. Bringing this program to Kingsley High School will have an invaluable impact on our students.

_____

_____

_____

_____

Were your comments for examples A and B different from example C? Examples A and B clearly exaggerate the effectiveness and impact of the programs being described. One program is not going to *change the face* of anything, especially by creating a *contagious atmosphere.* Very few programs are *one-of-a-kind*, and stating that your program will be is pompous and arrogant. Both examples A and B are clearly describing programs that are overexaggerated and, more than likely, unfunded by any grant-reviewing panel.

Example C, however, is written much more convincingly than examples A or B, but a few changes are still needed to eliminate any hyperbole or unspecific outcomes. The two words that we would change in example C are *incredible* and *invaluable.* Read the following revised example C, and notice how we still describe the program as having *incredible* results and an *invaluable* impact without using either term:

The students at Kingsley High School want to start a Model United Nations program after school. This nationally recognized program and curriculum has recorded consistent results centered on growth in student leadership, public speaking, and college acceptance rates when compared to students who did not participate in the program. By using this proven programming at Kingsley High School, we believe that the nationally published results can also take place with our students.

When writing initial drafts of your proposal, you will undoubtedly use some vague or grandiose terms. We get it; you are excited and energetic about your program! Just make sure to go back, highlight the *incredible* terms, and revise them, focusing on actual facts or research in your final draft.

Tip 6: Offend No One

As you are beginning to see, it is very important to be meticulous in your word choice when writing a grant proposal. When choosing your words, make sure there is no chance that you will offend anyone on the grant-reviewing panel. One slip could cost you the funding you desperately need.

Even the most articulate authors can make a blunder every once in a while, but in education, there are a few areas to pay close attention to. The first is when writing for your school's special education department. Always take the student-first approach, identifying the student first and then the disability, like this: students with special needs, students with individualized education plans, or a student who has a disability. Other terms to describe students with mental or cognitive disabilities can easily be offensive to educators and noneducators alike, so use your common sense with your diction. The politically correct terminology in the field of special education is constantly changing, so we definitely recommend consulting a special education teacher or your school's case manager to find out if some of the terminology you use in your proposal could be considered offensive.

Next, tread lightly when speaking of socioeconomic status. Referring to students as *poor kids* or communities as *bad neighborhoods* can also strike the wrong chord with members of the grant-reviewing committee. Certainly the inequalities and realities your students face need to be included in your proposal (see chapter 3, "What Is a Needs Statement?" section), but stick to descriptors such as *low-income, free and reduced lunch,* and *underprivileged.* These will be less likely to offend anyone on the reviewing panel in the way that negatively charged words, such as *poor, bad,* or *worst,* do.

When the grant-reviewing committee makes its final decision, seemingly small words can leave a big impact in favor of or against a proposal. Make sure you do not give the review panel any opportunity to be negatively affected by your wording.

Tip 7: Use Your English Teachers

You already have great resources in your school or district: the English teachers! Although students may hate the red pen of the English teacher, consider it your best friend. Even if you are in an elementary school, there is probably someone with a strong English background or English endorsement in your building. If not, reach out to the high schools within the district. If you are considering writing grants (which you probably are because you are still reading this book), start to make friends with an English teacher in your building or district right now!

> If you are an English teacher, still ask for a colleague to help review your work, focusing on grammar and word usage, before you submit your final proposal. We are sure you are more than equipped to edit a grant proposal yourself, but a new set of eyes after you have spent countless hours writing the proposal can make a huge difference.

Tip 8: Evidence Based over Adjective Based

Adjectives are great for giving compliments and writing thank-you cards but *not* for describing projects or staff members in grant proposals. Adjectives, especially when used in excess, take away from the validity of a program or your expected outcomes. Too many adjectives make your content sound like opinions rather than facts based on evidence. Funders want to see programs that are clearly "good, great, grand, and wonderful" based on cited evidence or researched-based practices, not based on the adjectives themselves.

Don't get us wrong; we are not saying to eliminate all adjectives from your proposal. Just use them carefully, and explain why you chose to describe your program or staff member with that particular adjective. Check out some of the paired statements in the following and decide which statement best describes the project or staff member using an evidence-based model:

- The hard-working and dedicated staff at Freemont Junior High will put all of their effort into making the Read to Grow program an innovative and successful project.

- The teaching staff at Freemont Junior High who will be creating the Read to Grow curriculum have an average experience of eleven years of classroom teaching. The innovative Read to Grow program is based on the most recent research and published studies on teaching literacy to middle school students. The combination of experienced staff and research-based practices will ensure the success of this programming.

The staff at your school may very well be hard-working and dedicated, but that is merely your opinion until you provide concrete data. By citing that the staff has eleven years of experience, you turn your adjective-based opinion into an evidence-based fact. The adjective *innovative* was kept to describe the Read to Grow program and then explained how the program was new and researched based. Here is another example:

- My energetic and amazing students need a safe and fun outdoor facility to play during recess. The student-designed playground will be an asset to the entire school because it will be safe, colorful, and have academic games integrated throughout the playground equipment.

- Darell Hammond, chief executive officer of Kaboom!, cites several research studies in his recent article in the *Huffington Post* that directly correlate physical activity for elementary students with an increase in students' standardized test scores, as well as an increase in attention span and a decrease in misbehavior. The student-designed playground project will allow my energetic students the space needed to play during recess and also have a positive impact on their classroom learning. The outdoor facility that my students design will also have academic games and manipulatives integrated in the playground equipment.

The first statement wouldn't convince any grant-reviewing panel to fund a *safe and colorful* outdoor playground for *amazing students*. Every teacher is going to think that her or his students are *amazing*, so leave this common opinion out of the proposal. Focus on what can be proven based on evidence, research, or data. Including a credible source on the impact of physical activity in elementary students will take your "lovey-dovey, we-need-a-safe-playground" statement to an evidence-based argument that will convince the funding organization that your students will benefit from an outdoor facility.

Adjectives may be easier to throw in than evidence, and you may think you are helping your overall word count. This adjective-based shortcut, however, is

Anecdotal evidence, however, does have a place in grant proposals. Tips for using anecdotal evidence to enhance your proposal are described in more detail in chapter 3 under the "What Is a Needs Statement?" section. Just be sure to keep these tips about adjectives in mind when using anecdotal evidence.

an incredible, massive, horrible mistake that will ultimately leave your awesome, amazing, innovative project unfunded.

Tip 9: Data Always Trumps Common Knowledge

The grant-reviewing panel will want to see data and research to prove your claims, so when writing a grant proposal, data always trump common knowledge. Always. Certain beliefs of the school or goals of the school district may sometimes seem like common knowledge to everyone involved in that school community, but to the funder—an outsider—your common knowledge claims are simply unproven statements.

Let's say you are writing a proposal for new theater equipment and state-of-the-art upgrades to your existing auditorium. If you mention that parents want a new auditorium and theater equipment, the funding organization is going to want to know how you arrived at that conclusion. The fact that parents support upgrades to the theater department may be common knowledge around your school or community, but it is not common knowledge to the funder. Your statement becomes weak, undocumented, anecdotal evidence. How do you know that parents want an upgraded auditorium? Is it simply from conversations with a few individual parents or a couple e-mails from the father of the lead student in the upcoming musical, or did you have parents fill out a survey about upgrades to the auditorium? What constitutes proof of your claims?

One of the most common ways to turn common knowledge into a statistical statement is to give a quick survey to all of the participants. For the previous example, a short, four- to five-question survey could be given to parents over the phone, at the next open house, or even online. The results from this survey (assuming they prove your common knowledge claim to be true) can be used as data to support your anecdotal evidence. A piece of common knowledge in the grant world is, no data, no funds, so just remember: if you make a statement supporting your proposal, make sure you have evidence to keep it from being uncommon knowledge.

Tip 10: Consistency

When you are writing a grant, you are most likely not going to sit down and write the entire proposal at that moment. Depending on the size of the grant, it usually will take multiple days or weeks (sometimes months) to complete your proposal. For larger grants, you will also be working with a team of teachers and administrators, and different sections of the proposal will be written by a variety of collaborators.

In instances like this, when a proposal is written over an extended period of time or by many people, consistency becomes a major issue. We have seen many proposals morph into choppy, short essays haphazardly pieced together. The key to fixing this inconsistency is time. Just as time is needed for editing the grammar and word choice, it is also needed to make sure the proposal is consistent in all of its descriptions.

Keeping the writing style, word usage, and program description consistent throughout the proposal is one of the greatest challenges you may face as you begin to assemble work teams and tackle RFPs. As you continue reading this book, consistency will be stressed multiple times. Right now, though, before you begin writing, make sure you have a clear picture of your project and a focused implementation plan. Discrepancies in the details of your program will leave the reviewing panel confused and unsure of your ability to carry out an organized and effective project.

> Keeping the writing style, word usage, and program description consistent throughout the proposal is one of the greatest challenges you may face.

Word and Character Counts Count

When the parentheses at the end of a prompt in the RFP say, "maximum five hundred words," it literally means do not write more than five hundred words! Word and character counts are not just suggestions for how long your proposal section should be; they are explicit rules that you must follow. Many grant writers tend to think of word or character counts as a speed limit sign: "speed limit 55." Most of us don't think that going 56, 57, or even 60 miles per hour is speeding, but with grant writing, having 501 words in a 500-maximum word zone is breaking the law! (See figures 2.1 and 2.2.)

Many foundations and companies that offer grant awards will have an online submission process in which you type your proposal into specific text boxes on their website (see figure 2.3). Many times, when you are using this type of grant proposal–submission process, you will not be allowed to type over the word or character count. Your ability to type will simply cease in that text box or window. In other cases, if you are typing your proposal submitting via e-mail or mailing a hard copy, it is your responsibility to honor all word and character counts. Often, before your proposal even gets in front of the review panel, it will be scanned by a team to make sure you have met all the requirements of the RFP; one of those requirements is the word or character count! If you are over the maximum, there is a good chance that your proposal will never even be read by the grant-reviewing panel.

As we break down the common sections included in most RFPs, we will make sure to remind you to watch your word or character count and give you some hints for how to prioritize all the information you want to include in each section.

Checking word and character counts is a very simple process on most word processors. If you are using Microsoft Word, you can check the entire word or character count by clicking "Tools" at the top of your screen and selecting "Word Count." A separate box will appear on your screen, breaking down your page, word, character, paragraph, and line counts (see figure 2.1).

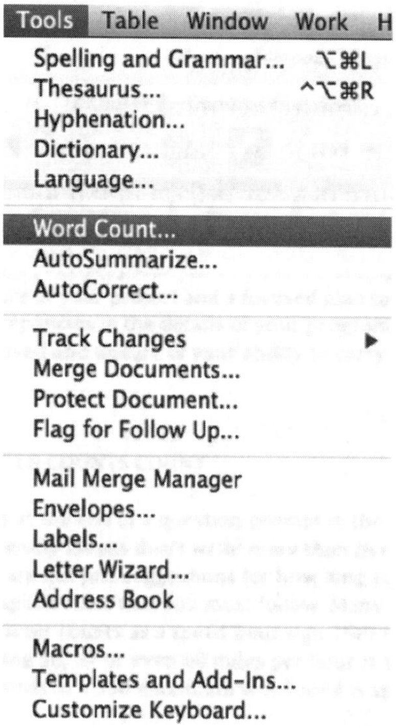

Tools	Table	Window	Work	H
Spelling and Grammar...			⌥⌘L	
Thesaurus...			^⌥⌘R	
Hyphenation...				
Dictionary...				
Language...				
Word Count...				
AutoSummarize...				
AutoCorrect...				
Track Changes			▶	
Merge Documents...				
Protect Document...				
Flag for Follow Up...				
Mail Merge Manager				
Envelopes...				
Labels...				
Letter Wizard...				
Address Book				
Macros...				
Templates and Add-Ins...				
Customize Keyboard...				

FIGURE 2.1 Word Count Menu

If you want to count the words or characters of a specific section of text, highlight the text you want counted, and then do the same procedure as before. This time only the words, characters, paragraphs, and lines of the highlighted text will be counted (see figure 2.2).

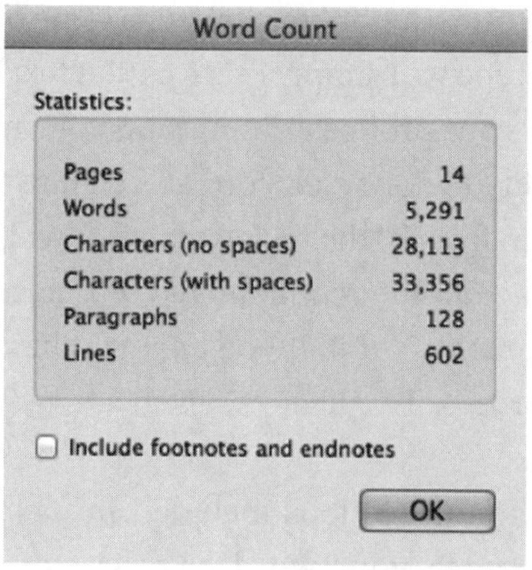

Word Count

Statistics:

Pages	14
Words	5,291
Characters (no spaces)	28,113
Characters (with spaces)	33,356
Paragraphs	128
Lines	602

☐ Include footnotes and endnotes

OK

FIGURE 2.2 Word Count Feature

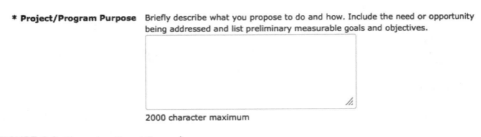

FIGURE 2.3 Character Count Example

Assemble Your Editing Team before You Start Writing

That statement may seem like a paradox. "Why would I need to assemble an editing team before there is anything for them to edit?" There are a lot of reasons! One is common courtesy. Giving your editing team plenty of advanced notice of deadlines and meetings will greatly increase the level of your editing team's commitment to your proposal. Furthermore, if you have your editing team in place early on in the process, you can give them each a section of your proposal to edit as you complete it. This will help the editing team pay closer attention to each section and will also give you feedback before you have written your entire proposal.

The size of your editing team will depend on the size of your grant. If the grant is a short, three-question RFP for $500, you probably will only need one person to review your proposal before you submit it. If the RFP is lengthy, with multiple sections or is a multiyear project, a team of at least five reviewers would be appropriate. As stated previously, keep close tabs on your approaching deadline. Reviewers need time to read, internalize, and provide suggestions when editing your proposal. Don't expect your editing team to stop everything they are doing and give you a complete and professional review three hours before you have to submit your proposal. (Trust us, we have tried to do it before. That grant proposal was not funded.)

Major Components of Most RFPs

You are almost ready to start writing! Before you begin, though, we want to take a moment to introduce the four major components of most RFPs. These four components are pretty standard in any type of grant. Each RFP will be unique and may offer a variance of prompts based on these components, but if you learn the ins and outs of writing for these general sections, you will be able to handle any question an RFP throws your way.

You should still have those RFPs we asked you to find in chapter 1. Try to identify each of the major components listed in the following in the RFPs you found.

Needs Statement or Statement of Need

The needs statement section of the proposal asks you to identify the root problem or problems facing your school or district in relation to your overall proposal. If you are requesting funds for technology, your needs statement should describe how your school's lack of technology is affecting student learning. The needs statement solidifies in the funder's mind the rationale for your request for money. More in chapter 3!

Project or Program Description

Also described in chapter 3, the project or program description is the "meat" of your proposal. Sometimes this section will contain multiple questions related to goals, instruction, implementation, and development. Take pride in your program and describe it to the funder with enthusiasm and commitment.

Budget

One of the most common yet feared sections of a grant proposal. We will go in depth on how to create and rationalize a budget in your proposal. Funders want to see how each dollar will be spent, but also how you will be gathering other nonmonetary support to be combined with their committed funding to complete the program. Don't worry; we got you covered in chapter 4!

Assessment and Evaluation

One of the more advanced components of implementing a funded proposal. The assessment and evaluation pieces are crucial to receiving initial funding, but also for future funding and the longevity of your program. Chapter 5 will make sure you are prepared to explain and take on assessing and evaluating your program.

Once you have the knowledge and skills to tackle these four common sections of any RFP, you will be able to churn out winning grants with more confidence and precision. Let's not waste any more time!

Second-Period Review Guide

✎ Be fully prepared before you sit down to write your grant. Gather data and resources pertaining to your school or district and specific information about your proposed program.

✎ Follow the ten writing tips while creating your proposal:
- Think of your proposal as a conversation with another teacher.
- Consider whether you want to use the first or third person.
- Your proposal is alive and active!
- Leave the slang on the streets.
- Your project is not "out of this world!"
- Offend no one.
- Use your English teachers.
- Make sure your points are evidence based over adjective based.
- Data always trump common knowledge.
- Be consistent.

✎ All ten writing tips must be used together to create your writing style.

✎ Keep track of your word and character counts.

✎ Assemble your editing team early.

✎ Four main components of most RFPs:
- Needs statement or statement of need
- Project or program description
- Budget
- Assessment and evaluation

Second-Period Exit Ticket

1. *True or false:* It doesn't matter if you use the first or third person, as long as you keep the point of view the same throughout the entire proposal.

2. *True or false:* You should assemble an editing and reviewing team before you even begin to write your proposal.

Third Period: Creative Writing

You do not need to be an experienced dissertation writer or an editor of a recognized periodical to write and win a grant. Teachers already possess several qualities that make them ideal candidates to write grants, especially grants that focus on providing students with a creative project or new experience. You know what your students need, you know the problems they face, and we hope you have an understanding of what it will take to make an impact on your students' learning experiences. In this chapter, you will find the basics of writing three vital components of your proposal: the needs statements, goals and objectives, and project descriptions. After breaking down each section, you will have the chance to read and critique a few examples from submitted proposals.

> Teachers already possess several qualities that make them ideal candidates to write and win grants.

What Is a Needs Statement?

A needs statement, sometimes called a *statement of need*, is the portion of your proposal in which you convince the granting organization that there is in fact a problem that needs to be addressed through your grant. A needs statement is more than a complaint; it is, as the name identifies, a statement—a statement that is supported by data and research and identifies a specific problem or challenge that you are going to tackle for the benefit of your students, school, district, or community.

The needs statement is the rationale behind your entire proposal. Think of a lesson plan. You see that your students are still not grasping long division, so you decide to create a lesson to review and practice long division. Every teacher will answer these questions when planning a reteaching lesson:

What is the problem? "My students have not mastered long division."

How do you know this? "According to my students' scores on their long division quiz, 90 percent of them received a grade below 70 percent."

Are there any other outside factors that may be also causing this problem? "Last year this group of students had three teachers during the academic year. Their first teacher left on maternity leave. The replacement quit after one month of teaching. The third teacher was a brand-new teacher and had several classroom management issues. With all of this mobility, the students did not master all the fundamental math concepts needed as a prerequisite for long division."

When combined, the answers to these questions would be the needs statement of this lesson plan. In this example, the teacher is stating a problem, using data to support the reality of the problem, and giving the reader some anecdotal evidence after research about some of the underlying causes. These three skills (identifying a problem, collecting and analyzing data about the problem, and researching the causes and effects of the problem) are all skills that teachers, including *you*, already possess, and these are the same skills needed to write a needs statement.

Many times needs statements are not considered an essential component of the proposal. Big mistake! As educators, we may think that a needs statement is obvious or implied. "Of course schools need money. State budget allocations to schools are being cut and property values are on the decline." However, the needs statement is your first, and sometimes only, chance to really explain the specific problem you or your students are facing.

Pretend for a moment you are the one who decides the winning proposal for a $1,000 classroom project grant. After you decide which teacher and classroom you think should win the $1,000, you have to justify the decision to your board of directors. How will you justify your choice? How will you convince the board that the $1,000 will be more beneficial to students in the grant proposal you chose versus the other submissions?

That is why the needs statement section is so vitally important to a winning proposal and cannot be put to the side or hastily written. You are essentially telling the granting organization the entire scope of the problem. The granting organization will justify their allocation of funds based on the greatest impact for the greatest need, so identifying and describing your problem will allow the granting organization to determine the total impact your proposal can make. Your plan to fix the problem—the project description (described later in this chapter)—is an equally important factor in determining funding. However, without a true sense of the problem being addressed, the granting organization will not be able to justify funding any project, no matter how great of a project or program is proposed.

Every needs statement should contain most, if not all, of the following information. Use this checklist as you view some completed needs statements in this chapter and in appendix A.

☐ Clear explanation of the problem or challenge facing the proposer

☐ Insight into the classroom, school, school district, and community with current student and school data

☐ Anecdotal evidence that allows the reader to connect to the proposer's students and school

☐ Data and research to support the problem, challenge, and anecdotal evidence

☐ Connection to a larger-scale problem or consequence (national research or statistics of what happens if the problem is not addressed)

What Types of Problems Can Be Identified and Described in a Needs Statement?

Short answer: the request for proposal (RFP) will tell you. Some RFPs will be very specific and require the proposal to address an already-stated problem or need.

> *Example:* "Projects should increase college-acceptance rates in students from public high schools in Oakland, California."

In this example, the problem is already implied—low college-acceptance rates among public students attending schools in Oakland, California. Your needs statement in a proposal for this RFP won't need to identify a new problem but should focus on describing how this problem is affecting your classroom and school. What is the college-acceptance rate at your school? What are some specific factors unique to your school that can be attributed to this problem?

In other cases, the RFP may be very broad, giving you more autonomy in addressing a problem that you identify. If this is the case, you will definitely need to do some research on the granting organization. Go online and read the mission and vision statement for the granting organization. What is the overall mission of the organization? What types of grants did they award in the previous fiscal year? Submitting a proposal about a project to engage students in an after-school drama club to a granting foundation that focuses on math and science advancement in the classroom may be a waste of your time.

Most RFPs do have some focus given to a specific area of interest. They may not be as specific as the previous example, but the RFP may state a focus such as, "Funds will be given to a teacher who plans and implements a classroom project to increase student literacy skills." Here the general problem has been identified for you—a deficiency in literacy skills among students in a teacher's classroom. Your needs statement for this RFP, then, should focus specifically on the literacy attributes of your students. How many of your students are below grade level?

What resources does your classroom lack that are needed to increase student literacy? You can also talk about your class size or the number of students with learning disabilities, from low-income households, or who are English language learners. All of this information will give the funder a clear picture of the "needs" in your classroom specific to the parameters set by the RFP.

Here are examples from education grant RFPs that ask the proposer to identify and explain the area of need. Notice how some of these RFP examples already identify the problem and others leave the identifying to the proposer.

> *Example one:* Describe your classroom. What needs do your students have? How will this project address those needs? (UNITE Classroom Grant)
>
> *Example two:* What problem does your project address? Why is this issue significant? Why is this a problem? (Carnegie Foundation, Urban and Higher Education Grant)
>
> *Example three:* Please provide evidence that the program or project responds to a valid need and is superior to other competing programs or projects. (Entertainment Software Association Foundation Youth Grant)

What Data Are Appropriate to Be Included in a Needs Statement?

For classroom or school-based proposals, most data and research you will use in your needs statement are already at your disposal and should be included, because many funders will be looking for information about your students or school. Most of this information can be found on your school or district website or from your school secretary, clerk, or administrative assistant. Most of this information is also listed on a school's state report card. Possible data may include the following:

- Student demographic data
- Student socioeconomic data
- Student mobility rates
- Student data from standardized tests
- Student attendance data
- Student behavior incident reports and data
- Student drop-out rates
- Teacher attrition rates
- Average experience level of teachers

Remember, you are trying to convince the funder that there is a substantial and documented need within your classroom, school, or district. Using data and research can help the reviewers of your proposal grasp the urgency and volume of the need at hand. Take the two following examples. Which one do you think shows a greater need?

- My fifth-grade students are reading at a second-grade level. This is a major problem for our classroom. My students will continue to fall behind if they cannot read at the appropriate grade level.

- Nineteen of my twenty-six students are reading below grade level, with twelve of these students more than three grade levels behind in reading. According to research by the Center for Public Education, students who are behind in reading in elementary school are four times more likely to drop out of high school.

Just stating that your fifth-grade students read at a second-grade level is not enough to create the recognition of a substantial need from a funder. Although fifth-grade students reading at a second-grade level indicated incongruency, you need to explain why it is also a big problem. The second example starts to paint a picture of the needs in your classroom to the funder; the funder sees that you have a classroom of twenty-six students, with the majority of them struggling to read. The second example also brings a respected source into the conversation about the larger scope of the problem and how students reading below grade level in fifth grade can lead to further problems.

Using Anecdotal Evidence in the Needs Statement

Anecdotal evidence can be a great asset to any proposal when used in moderation. Although this type of data doesn't contain facts and figures, it can give the funder more information about the needs of the population being served. Sometimes, a national statistic or research study followed by a quick anecdotal insight from your personal classroom can really help the reader make a connection to your students or staff.

Let's take a look at the following needs statement. This statement was adapted from a proposal submitted by a student teacher in Chicago for a $500 classroom project grant. Look closely at how she uses anecdotal evidence:

I am a student teacher in a kindergarten classroom in a K–8 elementary school in Chicago. In my class, there are twenty-one students, twelve of whom are ELLs with Spanish as their native language. My students will be beginning a unit on plants and the plant cycle next semester. My students are fortunate that they have access to some English resources inside the classroom; however, the ELL students don't have access to many books to read about plant life in Spanish. Although my cooperating teacher and I can speak and teach in Spanish, it does not have the same effect as reading a text. The students also don't have many opportunities for a hands-on-experience with plant life because most of them live in apartment buildings or condos where having a garden is not likely. My students lack the resources needed in order to get a full learning experience with plants.

The anecdotal evidence (students living in apartment buildings) used in this needs statement gives the reader some very important information about the needs of the students. This evidence could be made more valid with a few small pieces of statistical data to have a greater effect. For example, this student teacher could send a short survey home with each of her students asking parents or guardians to identify what type of building they live in and the number of plants in the house.

Here is an example of a simple survey this student teacher could have sent home. (Note that this student teacher's students are kindergartners, which is why a survey probably should be sent home. Depending on the information being collected, middle school or high school students could take the survey themselves.)

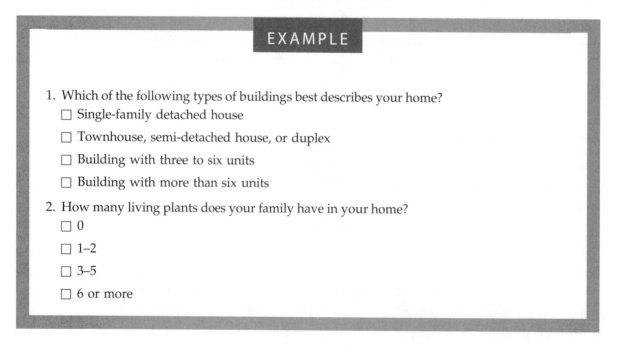

EXAMPLE

1. Which of the following types of buildings best describes your home?
   ☐ Single-family detached house
   ☐ Townhouse, semi-detached house, or duplex
   ☐ Building with three to six units
   ☐ Building with more than six units
2. How many living plants does your family have in your home?
   ☐ 0
   ☐ 1–2
   ☐ 3–5
   ☐ 6 or more

The answers to this simple survey can be used in conjunction with anecdotal evidence to strengthen your needs statement. Throw in some current and relevant research and you have just written a winning needs statement!

. . . students also don't have many opportunities for a hands-on-experience with plant life because 87 percent of my students live in a building that contains three or more housing units and do not have a yard for a garden. According to a recent survey of my students' parents and guardians, 67 percent of my students have zero living plants in their house and 22 percent only have one or two live plants. According to education author Cindy Middendorf, children ages four through seven need hands-on learning experiences to assist in the development of the right side of the brain. This development is crucial for students in kindergarten through second grade . . .

What If the Grant Application Does Not Ask for a Needs Statement?

Some education grants, especially grants that focus on teacher training or teacher travel, may not have a specific section dedicated to addressing the need. If this is the case, it is still important to give the funder an idea of how your project will work toward filling a deficiency. While describing your project in the proposal, make some references as to why this project is important to the population being served.

> *Example:* The "Read to Remember" program will increase student comprehension skills in both fiction and nonfiction texts. Last year on our school's end-of-the year assessment, 79 percent of fourth-grade students scored below proficient in reading comprehension skills.

Although not as detailed as a full needs statement, this one sentence will give a quick glance into one of the problems that this program will address.

Here is another example from a teacher travel grant in which the grant writers give the funder a brief needs statement under a different section called "Benefits to Teacher."

This entire grant proposal appears in the appendix as an example of a teacher travel grant. This proposal was funded and both teachers were able to visit South Africa at no cost to them!

The impulse for this project is that we teach in an embattled inner-city community. Our students are all black, and the community that surrounds the school is 98 percent African American. My colleague and I are both white and we struggle to find common ground with the families who send their children to our school. Obviously as Americans and as stakeholders in the future lives of their students we have a connection, but otherwise there is a clear cultural gap between us and this community. We believe that we can bridge this gap, however, by immersing ourselves in the root culture of African peoples, and by determining for ourselves the inspiration and inherent motives that inspire black communities back home.

The writers of this proposal are able to clearly outline a specific problem and give the funder a picture of the teachers' students, school, and community. This is a great example of giving the granting organization a needs statement without having been asked for one.

Needs Statement Wrap-up

Let's go back to the first example about low college-acceptance rates of students from public schools in Oakland, California. In this RFP, projects are being requested to increase college-acceptance rates in this school district.

> We hope you have gathered by this time that if your program does not directly affect students from Oakland, California, you should not even write a proposal for this RFP.

Here is the sample question that may be posed in this sample RFP:

Please identify root causes of students who do not get accepted into a four-year college on graduation from high school.

Following is an example of a complete, well-written needs statement based on the sample question. Let's use this example to review a completed needs statement. Don't forget to use the checklist at the beginning of this chapter as you read this needs statement.

Notice that in this needs statement the proposer does not tell the funder how he or she is going to increase college-acceptance rates (that comes in the next sections); the author is just painting a complete picture of the causes and problems of low college-acceptance rates.

Several causes exist for the 34 percent college-acceptance rate among graduating seniors at George Washington High School in Oakland, California. Located in one of Oakland's poorest communities, over 95 percent of George Washington High School students come from low-income households. According to the 2010 United States Census, in this community 53 percent of the residents identified as African American and 40 percent identified as Hispanic. Over 92 percent of families also reported as having incomes below the poverty line in 2010. These statistics only paint a portion of the picture of the inequalities students at George Washington High School face on a daily basis.

Many of the students work after school to help support their family income and in a recent survey given to all 389 seniors at George Washington High School, 78 percent reported spending one to three hours a day watching their younger siblings at home without any other adult present. These time commitments outside of school to support their family cut into students' time for homework and after-school college-enrichment opportunities.

Students entering George Washington High School as freshmen on average are three years behind in reading and four years behind in math compared to the average California freshman student as reported by the state education report card. The average GPA for students who graduate from George Washington but do not get accepted into a four-year college was 1.89 and the average SAT score was 956, far below the national SAT average of 1509 as reported by USA Today. These statistics also decrease the students' chances of being accepted into a four-year college. Based on the most recent report from the National Association for College Admissions Counseling, test scores and high school grades make up the top factors for college acceptance.

A lack of community members who were accepted into a four-year college and ultimately graduated is a major factor on the potential for growth and advancement of the Oakland community and its future students. Students who attend even two years of college are less likely to end up on government welfare and less likely to have a criminal record than students who never attend postsecondary education.

Let's review each step of the checklist in reference to this needs statement. Write down your notes on the lines provided after each check point.

☐ *Clear explanation of the problem or challenge facing the proposer*
Did this needs statement give you a clear picture of the low acceptance rate and some of its root causes specific to students at George Washington High School?

_____

_____

_____

_____

_____

☐ *Insight into the classroom, school, school district, and community with current student and school data*

What insight did you gain about the students in this school? What do you learn about the district? Can you describe the student population and the community demographics?

_____

_____

_____

_____

_____

☐ *Anecdotal evidence that allows the reader to connect to the proposer's students and school*

What information does the proposer give that is not supported by data or research but helps you connect to the students, school, or community?

_____

_____

_____

_____

_____

☐ *Data and research to support the problem, challenge, and anecdotal evidence*

List some data and research that are given to support the problem of low college-acceptance rates. How does this proposal use data and research to strengthen even some of the anecdotal evidence? What credible sources are citied?

_____

_____

_____

_____

_____

☐ *Connection to a larger-scale problem or consequence (national research or statistics of what happens if the problem is not addressed)*

How does the writer connect this problem at George Washington High School to a broader issue and problem? What will most likely happen if this problem persists?

_____

_____

_____

_____

_____

We hope this example and reviewing exercise gave you a chance to review and summarize all the information presented in this chapter about needs statements. Don't forget to check out appendixes A and B for examples of needs statements and full grant proposals!

Writing Goals and Objectives

As a teacher, you write multiple objectives every day. Each lesson plan has one to two objectives and clear, measureable outcomes that can be achieved within a class period or at the end of a class project. Teachers also make goals for their students and for themselves. Like in your classroom, goals and objectives play a critical role in grant writing.

Objectives and goals are very different. Goals are long-term, overarching targets that can be reached by continuous dedication and preference. Objectives are outcomes that can be measured within a given time frame. A series of objectives help you keep focused and strive for the overall goal. Sometimes goals can be achieved, and sometimes goals are simply ideal situations that continue to motivate. The following is an example of a classroom goal versus a focused daily objective:

> _Goal:_ 100 percent my students will be reading on grade level by the end of the year.
> _Daily objective:_ Students will be able to place events from a nonfiction text in chronological order.

Here the goal is a lofty one, but it can be achieved. The daily objective is a focused, measurable step along the path to reach the goal of all students reading on grade level.

When writing educational grants, you will have to distinguish among stating goals, objectives, or both in your proposal. Your project's goals and objectives should be in direct response to your proposal's needs statement. If your needs statement identifies a lack of arts and enrichment at your school, your goals and objectives should present some sort of clear improvements to the arts and enrichments programming.

Each section of your proposal has to fit together! If you identify a problem, how are you going to make it better?

Goals versus Objectives

The majority of the time, when you apply for classroom or school-based grants under $5,000, the funders will want objectives for a specific program or project. In most of these cases, the funding organization assumes that your "goal" is the same as the school's, which we hope is educating and improving the lives of children. However, a funder will most likely ask for you to list your goals if you are proposing an outside school program for the community, traveling out of the school's community, partnering with multiple organizations, or writing a multi-year proposal.

> This is a great time to mention again that each RFP is unique. If you find yourself unsure about including goals or objectives in your proposal, you can call the granting organization and ask to speak to the program officer about the proposal. Many organizations that offer grants will have a contact person, including contact information within the RFP. Don't be afraid to take advantage of this and reach out for clarity.

If you are writing the goal of your project, program, or trip, make sure that it is aligned to the granting organization's mission statement or organizational goals and values. It is a great idea to use some of the funder's own language in your proposal. This will show that you have done your research and will make a clear connection between the goal of your program and the mission of the granting organization.

Remember that a goal is the long-term outcome. Your proposal may not be able to achieve your goal. You may need to search for funds to buy sticky notes, chart paper, markers, and thirty copies of a novel to complete a reading unit. More than likely, this one unit or project will not be able to achieve a goal of 100 percent of students reading at grade level, but it can be a great project to help students grow toward achieving that goal and meet several smaller objectives in the given time frame.

This is why most smaller classroom grants will not specifically ask you for goals, but they will ask you for objectives for your specific unit or project. Unit plan objectives are great places to start when thinking about what objectives to include in your proposal.

Five Essentials for Writing Objectives

- *Alignment:* Much like writing a goal, your objectives should also be aligned to the granting organization's overall mission. Even if the RFP is fairly open, make sure your project fits within the broader context of what the funder has approved in previous years.

- *Participants:* Make sure the participants are mentioned in your objectives. How many students or participants? What grade or age?

- *Time:* How long will this project last from beginning to end?

- *Results:* What outcomes and results are expected to be achieved? Be specific!

- *Measurable:* How will you measure the outcomes? How will you know if the project or program worked as you proposed?

Take a moment to review the following objectives. Each of these objectives is missing one or two of the essential components we discussed. See if you can identify which essential component(s) are missing. (For this exercise, assume that each of the following objectives is aligned to the granting organization's mission.)

> *Objective A:* During my four-week poetry unit, each student will show an increase in prose recognition and rhythmic stanzas recognition. I will measure this by giving my students a preassessment at the beginning of the unit and a postassessment at the conclusion of the unit.

What is missing?

_____

_____

_____

_____

_____

> *Objective B:* Each of my twenty-four sixth-grade students will increase their overall math grade-level score by at least 20 percent during Saturday Math Academy. Students will be tested using the National Advancement for Math Curriculum pre- and postassessments for sixth-grade students.

What is missing?

_____

_____

_____

_____

_____

> *Objective C:* Students at Madero Middle Academy will become better students and citizens.

What is missing?

_____

_____

_____

_____

_____

How do you think you did?

Objective A is missing two key components: participants and specific results. In objective A, there is no mention of the number of students or participants or their grade level or age. Remember, funders want the biggest impact for their dollar, so make sure to give them the number of people who will achieve your objective. Objective A does mention that students will *increase* in certain literature skills, but the increase is not specific. To a funder, the word *increase* needs to be accompanied by specific numbers, such as, "Students will increase 5 points or 20 percent from their pre- to postassessment." Your specific results don't have to include an increase. The results can be an average score of all participants or even a decrease in discipline marks or referrals, depending on your proposal.

Objective B is missing the time component. This objective does a great job of identifying the participants, the results, and how the project will be measured, but no time frame is given for the Saturday Math Academy. Is this Saturday program happening for one month? One quarter? One school year? Multiple school years? Is it happening every Saturday or every other Saturday? Placing a time frame in your objective will help the funder know exactly when the organization can expect the desired results to be obtained and, ultimately, if your project should be funded.

Objective C is just a mess. Objective C is phrased more like a long-term goal than a well-written objective. This objective is missing all five of the essential components. How many students? How old are these students? How long will the desired outcomes take to be achieved? How will becoming better students and citizens be measured? Becoming better students and citizens is technically a result, but it definitely needs to be more specific. Check out the following objective C after it was revised to meet all five of the essential components:

> *Objective C:* Through the *My Community, My World* project, all 739 students from fifth grade through eighth grade at Madero Middle Academy will show an average of a ten-point increase in citizenship aptitude during the sixteen-week project. Citizenship aptitude will be determined using a teacher-created assessment in partnership with graduate students from the University of Florida.

Where Do I Put My Goals and Objectives in the Proposal?

Some RFPs will have a specific section for you to list the goals and objectives of your proposal. However, most RFPs will ask you to address your goals and objectives within a major section of the RFP, such as the project description (more on this section later in this chapter). Here is an example of an RFP section from the Ezra Jack Keats Minigrant Program:

> *Statement I:* Project Description
> Provide a thorough description of your project, clearly stating what you and your students will do. Describe its objectives. Tell how your project is new or different.

In this RFP, the granting organization specifically asks you to *describe* your objectives. Make sure you don't just simply list your objectives but describe them as part of your project description. Go into more detail about how that objective will be measured or who will be participating. If an RFP does ask you to list your goals and objectives, bullet points or separate lines for each goal and objective are usually appropriate.

If an RFP makes no reference to your goals or objectives, it is still important to include them in some capacity in your proposal. Similar to the needs statement, try to work in your project objectives and outcomes into the meat of your program description. Even making a quick reference to each objective as you explain the results you hope to achieve is a great way to show the funder you have a clear focus and plan for your project or program.

The Project Description

The project description is usually recognized as the most important section of your proposal. Although we are not going to disagree with that statement, it is also important to note that, without an identified needs statement, clear goals and objectives, a focused budget, and a process for evaluating the entire project, the project description becomes simply a great idea instead of the keystone of the entire proposal.

Although every RFP may not ask for a needs statement or goals and objectives, every RFP will have a section asking you to describe your project in detail. This is your chance to tell the granting organization how you will fix or improve the problem you have identified. This is your chance to tell the funder exactly how you will achieve each of your goals. This is your chance to bring home the money!

Think of your proposal as a plot outline and the project description as the climax, the make-or-break point in your proposal when the conflict (needs statement) is resolved (see figure 3.1)!

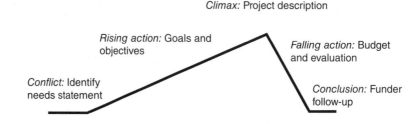

Climax: Project description

Rising action: Goals and objectives

Conflict: Identify needs statement

Falling action: Budget and evaluation

Conclusion: Funder follow-up

FIGURE 3.1 Grant Writing Plotline

Make sure to refer back to chapter 2 when writing your project description, paying close attention to first person versus third person, tone of voice, grammar usage, and word count!

Here are a few keys items for you to consider before writing your project description:

- *Keep track of your word or character count.* The project description usually contains the most information out of any section in your proposal, so it is easy to reach your word or character count without describing your entire program.

- *Make sure to address your needs statement.* The project description is the detailed explanation of how you are going to fix the problem you identified. You need to make sure that your description will make the funder agree that your program will be able to solve the problem addressed in your needs statement.

- *Pretend the funder knows nothing about you or your school.* Don't insult the granting organization by explaining basic knowledge terms (such as *math* or *assessment*), but be sure to explain terms such as *RTI, project-based learning,* or *differentiation.* More than likely, at least one person on the proposal review panel will not be familiar with some of the newest education terminology. Furthermore, by explaining these keys terms, you will prove to the funder that you know what you are talking about and not just throwing buzz words into your proposal.

- *Keep it consistent.* Your entire proposal must flow seamlessly into one consistent, coherent written work. Language you use in your needs statement, objectives, budget, and evaluation should make an appearance in your project description. If you mention a twelve-week time frame in your objective, make sure that same twelve-week time frame is referenced in your project description. If you have stipends for three teachers in your budget to run an after-school program, make sure you mention three teachers in your project description.

- *Don't exaggerate.* In the description of your program, stay away from fluffy words that tend to make your project sound like the cure for cancer, such as *earth-shattering, exponentially,* or *phenomenal.* **Note:** Go back to chapter 2 to review these and other words to shy away from in your proposal.

Start with the Basics

Who, what, where, when, why, and how questions must be answered here in the project description. It may sound obvious, but you need to let the funder know exactly what you are doing, who is doing it, where it is happening, and so on. The best way to start your project description is to make an outline of your answers to these six common questions. Here is an example outline of a proposal submitted about starting an after-school chess club:

> *Who:* Fourteen high school students and one teacher; ideally have students who either need a challenge or may have behavior problems and need an energy outlet
>
> *What:* Start an after-school chess club, possibly turn club into a future chess team or enrichment class
>
> *Where:* In my classroom, at my school
>
> *When:* Tuesdays and Thursdays after school from 3:30 PM until 4:10 PM
>
> *Why:* Increase critical-thinking skills of students and build student-to-student relationships
>
> *How:* Get funding, recruit students, hold informational meeting, build curriculum, teach chess and strategy, hold internal chess tournaments, have students reflect

This outline is only for you, so it doesn't have to be in perfect sentence structure or contain your final diction. This outline will serve simply as a guide for you to follow to make sure you include everything in your final project description. Beginning with the "five Ws and how" questions can really help you start to put your program idea down on paper. More than likely, your outline will change as you start to write your proposal and work through all the details of your program.

Other basics include the following:

- *Time:* Specify how long your project or program will last and exactly when each objective will be completed. This should match your time frame in your objectives.

- *Staff or instructors:* If your project is not necessarily a classroom project and will involve teachers, school staff, or volunteers other than yourself, it is important to include the title and number of other adults in your program. However, names are not necessary in the proposal.

  > *Example:* Four full-time classroom teachers employed at Martin Luther King Elementary and two adult parent volunteers will oversee the development and implementation of the Book Buddies program.

Chronological Implementation Plan

Your project description needs to answer all of the identified basic questions, but it also needs to be written in a logical, easy-to-follow time frame. Most funded proposals contain an implementation plan within the project description (or as a separate section, depending on the RFP). Your implementation plan is your step-by-step timeline of each activity in your project. This, too, may sound obvious, but careful attention needs to be given to how the project will be rolled out from start to finish. Much like outlining the basic who, what, where questions, you should also draft a timeline of each phase of your project, including every activity that will ultimately ensure that you achieve your stated objectives. Depending on the total time of your project, your outline should be in days, weeks, or months. For most classroom projects, you do not need to break down each daily lesson, but an overview of the curriculum on a week-by-week basis may be a necessary component. Following is one template you can use to jot down some of your implementation plan before writing your project description.

Project name: Dates: Materials:		
Week number	Activities	Meets objective number
1		
2		
3		
4		
5		

For any project, planning must take place before any actual implementation. Make sure whatever template you use to construct your implementation plan includes your planning stage in the first week or month. Examples of activities in the planning stage include lesson planning, buying materials, communicating with partnering organizations, making copies, hiring extra staff or securing volunteers, sending out parent memos, or attending a professional development training session.

Each component of your program should be planned out from the time you are notified of your award to the final communication with the granting organization. A project planned from start to finish will show your commitment and dedication to the funding organization.

Expanding Your Project's Impact

As stated previously in this chapter, funding organizations fund projects that align to their own mission and give them the greatest outcome based on the greatest need. In order to decipher this, funders will weigh the targeted population and number of people served by your program in their final decision. One way to give your project an advantage over other proposals is to increase the reach of your program. Many times this can be done without changing or adding to your project, but by simply explaining to the funder how your program will continue to make an impact after the initial objectives are completed.

For instance, let's say that you want to write a proposal to receive funding for twenty-five iPads for your classroom of twenty-five students. You will use these iPads for multiple class projects that you describe in your proposal. A way to make your proposal more attractive is to expand the reach of the requested iPads from your twenty-five students to more than five thousand people. How? Simple. Think about who can use the iPads when your students are not using them and how the iPads can be used in subsequent years.

Look at figure 3.2. The immediate participants are your twenty-five students. These students will complete the units and activities described in your proposal. However, as you follow the graphic outward, you can see the potential impact of your proposal for the entire school and community. In your project description, you can briefly describe that the other teachers at your grade level will use the iPads, that you will open up the iPads to the rest of the teachers at your school to use in their classrooms on Friday of each week, that the after-school literacy program that meets in your classroom on Tuesdays and Thursdays will use the iPads, and that the counselors who run an adult learning technology course will also have access to the iPads on Wednesday evenings. Now in one school year,

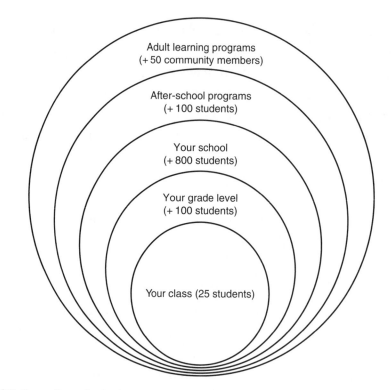

FIGURE 3.2 Expanding a Project's Impact

one thousand students and community members are being serviced by your proposal. Multiply that by five years and your idea to use iPads with your twenty-five students now has the potential to affect five thousand students and community members!

> Each year one thousand students and community members will be serviced by the iPads during various programs at school. Over the course of the next five years, roughly five thousand students and community members will have access to the iPads.

When measuring the longevity of technology, five years is usually a good projection of how long the technology will be relevant and make an impact. Although iPads or computers may service participants longer than five years, funders will usually see any projection over five years as a hypothetical to create a concrete argument.

Another way to expand your proposal's impact is to find an outside partner or stakeholder to partner with. Especially when writing a smaller classroom grant for a particular unit or project, stating that you will have an outside school partner will be a key feature in helping you expand your project's impact and distinguish you from the competition. Instead of just taking a field trip to a botanical garden after your project on Punnett squares and pollination, think of a way that your class can partner with the botanical garden throughout the year. Maybe a speaker from the botanical garden visits your classroom and facilitates a presentation for your students. Or maybe your class produces a video that is uploaded to the botanical garden website for the public to view. These types of partnerships with outside organizations will definitely propel your proposal to the top of the pile!

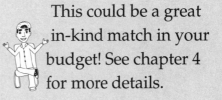 This could be a great in-kind match in your budget! See chapter 4 for more details.

Naming the Project

Large corporations have full-time staff to develop clever marketing strategies and eye-catching advertisements and publications. Unfortunately, schools don't have full-time staff for this purpose, but marketing and naming the project is a huge part of writing a winning proposal. Much like the needs statement, teachers already possess some inherent qualities that make them creative advertisers! Here are a few tricks to help you unleash your hidden marketing skills and make your proposal memorable to the reviewer panel.

Acronyms. A teacher's day is filled with acronyms! NCLB (No Child Left Behind), RTI (response to intervention), CCSS (Common Core State Standards), and SIP (school improvement plan) are just a few. Although trying to remember these acronyms may be a first-year teacher's biggest nightmare, acronyms are a great advertising tool when naming your project or proposal. If you can associate an acronym with your proposal, the chances of its being remembered by the reviewer panel will greatly increase. Your acronym should contain information describing the project, the participants, and the expected outcomes. Here are some examples of project titles that have been used in submitted proposals:

- **Project PLAY** (Planning Lifestyle Activities for Youth)
  A project to construct an outdoor area for students to play and learn during recess and after school
- **GET SCIENCE!** (Girl Empowerment Through Science Camp with Integrating the Enhancement of Newly Certified Educators)
  UNITE's summer programming designed to give new teachers experience in the classroom and provide a summer science camp for inner-city female students

- **PLANT** (Preserving and Learning About Nature Together)

  A class unit about plants, forest, and the depleting supply of forests throughout the world

- **IPAD** (Investing in Positive Academic Development)

  Funds requested for an iPad to use a specific application to track and record academic development of students with special needs

Play on words. Come up with a project title using a play on words that will give the reviewer some idea into your project's goals or activities. This may take you several brainstorming sessions, but in the end a catchy project title that uses a play on words will make a memorable impact. One such example was a proposal submitted by a special education teacher entitled *Dollars and $ense*. The project entailed students running a school store for their peers and working on future job-placement opportunities.

Stating outcomes in your subtitle. If you can't come up with an acronym or a play on words, being very direct about the project's outcomes in the subtitle of your project can have a similar effect. Come up with a short two- to four-word title, and then have your subtitle state the end result of your program; for example, *Truth or Dare: Empowering Students to Make Positive Decisions*. In this example, the reviewer will have a clear understanding of the objective of your project. The title's direct reference to your objective can help the reviewer focus on the end result as he or she reads through the entirety of your proposal.

Evaluation and the Project Description

Most likely, you will not include your evaluation process in the project description, because most RFPs will have a specific section for you to state your entire evaluation plan. One or two sentences in your project description stating that you are going to have an evaluation or assessment, along with a statement in your implementation plan explaining your time table for assessments, will add consistency to your proposal. However, going into more detail about the rationale for evaluation can many times take away from the activities outlined in your project description.

When reading through the RFP, make particular note to the words *evaluate* or *assess* in any of the given prompts. If there is not a specific question addressing the evaluation of your program, you may talk briefly about your evaluation process in either your project description or goals and objectives. See chapter 5 for more information about evaluating and assessing your project or program.

Examples of Project Description Prompts

As you have seen from the examples in this chapter, each RFP is unique; as you gain experience writing grant proposals, you will start to see how some sections overlap in RFPs and some are very distinct. Take a look at some examples of project description prompts in the following RFPs.

These RFPs would be a great place to start writing some smaller classroom grants! More information on each of these RFPs and several others can be found in appendix B of this book.

UNITE Classroom Grant RFP: Describe your project in detail. Have you done this project before? If so, what were the results? If not, where did you get the inspiration for this project? How will this project be aligned to one or more state standards? Will your project meet any of the three key components to a well-funded project (measurable student outcomes, inquiry and critical thinking, and service learning component)? (maximum of 1,000 words)

In the UNITE Classroom Grant RFP, the basic question, "Describe your project in detail," is asked, as well as other questions that also need to be answered. When writing a response to this prompt, be sure to include information you created in your outline and your implementation plan timeline, as well as answers to the specific questions addressed in the prompt. In a complex prompt like this, make sure to follow the order of the questions in the prompt. Describe your project, then describe if you have done it before, the inspiration, and so on. Sticking to the order of questions in a prompt will focus your response and make it easier for the reviewers to read and score your proposal.

Association of American Educators Classroom Grant RFP: Concise summary of classroom grant request. (150-word maximum)

This prompt doesn't sound like it is asking for a full project description, but with this RFP, it is! The Association of American Educators Classroom Grant is another small classroom grant award of up to $500 for a classroom unit or project. The RFP asks for you to summarize your request in only 150 words! Later on in this RFP, you have a chance to describe a lesson plan that "clearly demonstrates how the items will be used effectively in the classroom and how they will promote effective student learning." Your 150-word summary should stick to answering the basic questions, giving a very brief implementation plan. Finding

> This paragraph, from "This prompt" to "character counts" is 146 words!

other sections of the RFP to include more details about instruction, student needs, the extended impact of your proposal, and your goals and objectives is a strategy that experienced grant writers rely on to overcome word and character counts.

ING Unsung Heroes Awards Program RFP: Provide a thorough description of your project, clearly stating what you and your students will do. Describe its objectives. Tell how your project is new or different.

This prompt is very similar to the Ezra Jack Keats Minigrant Program prompt that was included earlier in this chapter. In this prompt, the funding organization is directly asking you to include and describe the objectives within your project description. Similar to the UNITE Classroom Grant prompt, follow the order given in the prompt. Write a thorough description with your implementation plan and extended impact, then describe your objectives, and finally state how your project is new or different.

Following is a section from the Walmart Foundation Community Giving RFP. Notice how in this RFP, the project description has been divided into distinct sections. This RFP is asking for much of the same information as the UNITE RFP or ING Unsung Heroes RFP, but it is clearly divided making it easier for the writer to follow. Also note how the program description is just a brief overview of the program.

Program description (paragraph, 2,000-character maximum)	*Instructions:* A brief description of proposed program
Program goals (paragraph, 2,000-character maximum)	*Instructions:* Description of program goals and objectives (including target population and number of people impacted)
Implementation plan (paragraph, 2,000-character maximum)	*Instructions:* Plan to accomplish goals and objectives and timeline for implementation
Program distinctions (paragraph, 2,000-character maximum)	Descriptions of what sets your program apart from like programs serving the same need or population
Communication (paragraph, 2,000-character maximum)	Description of how the program, its progress, and outcomes will be communicated and with whom

Putting It All Together

Let's look at a modified project description created from the previously mentioned school chess club project description outline. As you read, complete the following tasks:

- Circle the answers to the basic questions (who, what, where, etc.).
- Underline the activities that the students will take part in to achieve the objectives.
- Place a star by any reference to time or dates.
- Place a box around the project title.

> The project, "Checkmate," is an after-school program focused on developing reasoning, problem solving, and positive social interactions by learning about the game of chess. I will announce the project to all of my sophomore classes with the intent of attaining at least fourteen students. Ideally they would include at least three special education students, three students who typically have behavioral issues, three students who are struggling academically, and five students who typically excel in my classroom and would benefit from extra challenges. We would all meet for forty minutes after school on Tuesdays and Thursdays. The overarching goal of "Checkmate" would be to develop invaluable intellectual and social skills through playing the game of chess. "Checkmate" would run for the last ten weeks of school and we hope to continue the following school year.
>
> For the first week, our time would entail thirty minutes of guided instruction including the history of chess, how to play, and the benefits of playing it. They would conclude with ten minutes to practice with the chess boards. This time would be used to become more comfortable with the game and executing its rules. By the second week, our students will be playing against one another practicing techniques gleaned from instruction for more than half of our time. Overall, the game of chess will be used as a vehicle to teach life skills. In an article from *The Benefits of Chess in Education*, Jerry Meyers describes multiple intellectual skills, such as focusing, thinking ahead, weighing options, and thinking abstractly, that are developed from playing the game of chess. Each session will emphasize the skills needed to play chess and the life skills one can acquire from playing chess.
>
> By documenting the academic performance and the behaviors of my students in "Checkmate" until the end of the academic

school year, I will be able to reliably determine the effect of learning chess on them. The reason for including the students who struggle academically is to track their academic performance until the end of the year and show an increase in test scores. The reason for at least three students with behavioral issues to participate is to track their behavior after participating in "Checkmate" and show a decrease in referrals, detentions, and suspensions. Critical thinking and problem-solving are skills learned in chess, but the increase in academic performance and good behavior are the measurable pieces that will illustrate the positive outcomes from this project.

In the proposed budget for "Checkmate," I have chosen a book entitled *The Everything Chess Basics Book*. Reading this book will be part of the instruction portion of the forty-minute time allotted after school. It will give the teacher the material to provide scaffolding for students who have never played chess. It will also provide specific techniques that inherently require critical thinking and questioning skills. *The Everything Chess Basics Book* will give our students a foundation on which they will build their chess skills with proper instruction from the teacher.

What did you circle? Did this teacher answer all the basic questions?

How many student activities did you underline?

How long was the program? How many stars did you place by reference to date and time in this proposal? When are the student activities taking place?

What was the project title? Did it catch your eye or give you a window into what the project would actually do?

After reading this project description, you should have a pretty clear idea about what will happen during the first few weeks of "Checkmate." The teacher will recruit a targeted number of students, meet twice a week after school for forty minutes, use a book to help teach the game of chess, and the students will get time to play against one another using the skills they learned. The author also makes references to his or her objectives (see the first sentence) and the overall goal to develop intellectual and social skills. A credible research source is cited, and this teacher also mentions what data he or she will be collecting and the rationalization for the targeted students and analysis.

Although this example does a decent job covering the basic components of a project description, the author does not give a detailed description of the project after week two. The project sounds like it will have a great foundation in the beginning weeks, but what is going to happen after week two through the end of the program? This is why mapping out your implementation plan before you begin the actual writing of your project description can prove useful.

This project description loses its chronological order narrative when the author jumps from activities in week two to citing an article on the benefits of chess and then talking about his or her assessment process. A better order would be for the article citation to appear toward the end of the first paragraph after the author stated the goals and objectives of "Checkmate."

The third paragraph also adds to the confusion in this project description, because it is a combination of secondary objectives and a rationale for evaluation. Depending on the other prompts in the original RFP, this paragraph could be eliminated and inserted into other sections of the proposal, either in the goals and objectives or evaluation and assessment.

Now, read the revised project description for "Checkmate," noticing how the description flows in a chronological order and gives a complete overview without clouding the description with misplaced content:

> The project, "Check-Mates," is an after-school program focused on developing reasoning, problem solving, and positive social interactions by learning about the game of chess and building new friendships or "mates." In an article from *The Benefits of Chess in Education*, Jerry Meyers describes multiple intellectual skills, such as focusing, thinking ahead, weighing options, and thinking abstractly, that are developed from playing the game of chess. Each session will emphasize the skills needed to play chess and the life skills one can acquire from playing chess.

> The project will be announced to all of my sophomore classes with the intent of attaining fourteen students. Ideally they would include at three special education students, three students who typically have behavioral issues, three students who are struggling academically, and five students who typically excel in my classroom and would benefit from extra challenges. We would all meet for forty minutes after school on Tuesdays and Thursdays. "Check-Mates" would run for the last ten weeks of this academic year and we hope to continue the following school year.

> Before the first after-school session of "Check-Mates," I will make informational handouts to recruit students, buy the chess boards and copies of the book entitled *The Everything Chess Basics Book*, and plan the first two weeks of after-school sessions. *The Everything Chess Basics Book* will serve as the textbook and will be part of the instruction portion of the forty minutes allotted after school. For the first week, our time

would entail thirty minutes of guided instruction including the history of chess, how to play, and the benefits of playing it. They would conclude with ten minutes to practice with the chess boards. This time would be used to become more comfortable with the game and executing its rules. By the second week, our students will be playing against one another practicing techniques gleaned from instruction for more than half of our time. Weeks three through seven will be the "regular season," in which a schedule will be created and students will play one another keeping a running record of their victories and losses. After each completed chess match, a one-page reflection essay will be written by each student reflecting on the game, their strategic choices, and their attitudes toward the game and their opponent. Weeks seven through nine will be the "playoffs" in which a round-robin style chess tournament will decide the winner of the "Check-Mate" program. Sportsmanship and reflection will be a focus during competition rounds. During the final week of the program the students will get to challenge a staff member from Truman High School in a game of chess. Fourteen staff members have already committed to playing the students in chess during the final week of the program.

The students will be continuously assessed and monitored throughout the program to make sure progress toward the previously stated objectives is being made. More information about the evaluation procedures and timeline can be found in the assessment and evaluation section of this proposal. Results from the project and personal reflection statements from each student participant will be shared with all stakeholders, including the granting organization. With success in this initial phase, "Check-Mates" will continue in subsequent years and expand to engage and affect more students across grade levels at Truman High School.

In this revised project description, the focus is clearly on the implementation of the project. It is described in chronological order, outlining the entire ten weeks of the programming, including the initial planning stages. The name of the program was changed to "Check-Mates" to highlight one of the objectives of positive social interactions while using a play on words. The last paragraph makes reference to the evaluation of the assessment but does not go into the rationale or specific assessment procedures.

Be confident and thorough when describing your program. Refer back to the ten writing tips in chapter 2 as often as needed. Take a deep breath and get started!

Third-Period Review Guide

✎ Your needs statement is an explanation of the problem or challenge facing your students, school, or district.

✎ Use data to support the claims in your needs statement.

✎ Connect your specific problem to a larger-scale consequence.

✎ Goals are long term; objectives are the short steps taken to reach the ultimate goal.

✎ Your project description is the climax of your proposal.

✎ Make sure your project description answers the who, what, where, when, why, and how questions.

✎ Have a focused chronological implementation plan.

✎ Expand the impact of your program and make it stand out by partnering with a community organization and having a memorable name.

Third-Period Exit Ticket

1. Which of the following must be included in a proficient needs statement?

   a. Clear explanation of the problem or challenge

   b. Insight into your classroom or school

   c. Data and research supporting your stated need

   d. All of the above

2. *True or false:* Every proposal should state the project's goal and some attainable objectives.

3. Define the implementation plan.

Fourth Period: Economics

You have now arrived at the part you have been waiting for. You have thought through your project, found a funder, and perhaps have even written some descriptions of your project or proposal. It is now time to match what you need to complete your project with how much it all costs.

In this section, we will discuss the stakeholders involved in writing, reviewing, and executing the financial components of your grant; identify the needs of your proposal and assign costs to them; create and present your own proposed budget; ascertain alternative routes to funding projects; develop budget narratives; provide money management techniques; and report financial activities of a project.

> We have provided flexibility in this section to include all levels of grant funding. As you read on, please be aware that every RFP is different and requires varying levels of detail. You may find that although some budgets are very simple, others require much more advanced techniques. When in doubt, always seek the assistance of a seasoned budget manager, including your school clerk, an administrator, or an outside source (business person, nonprofit leader, other project partner), or call the funders directly to clarify their needs. Oftentimes, program officers at granting organizations are more than happy to talk candidly about the requirements, because they want successful proposals to be submitted.

What Is a Budget?

When writing grants, budgets can take many forms. The simplest definition of a grant budget is *a plan for the coordination of resources and expenditures*. Let's break down this definition piece by piece.

A plan . . . With your proposal, you are developing a detailed plan of using the resources and funds available to you *over a set course of time*. As with your lesson plans, you must determine the length of your budget. If you are working on a small, one-time technology grant, for example, then your budget may cover only the semester or year. It may specify when you will purchase the equipment as well as more detailed information about that equipment.

If you are working on a larger grant, however, your budget may need to be broken down by semester, season, year, or other specified length of time. When determining the length of time, be sure to take into consideration (1) the requirements and limitations outlined in the RFP; (2) the relevance of that time frame to your project; (3) the operating cycles of your institution and any other partner organizations (i.e., academic or fiscal year calendars); and (4) the logistical and operational ramifications of your selected time frame.

Although setting a time frame may not be a major factor in many small grants, it plays an integral role in the success of larger grants that require multiple organizations to collaborate over many years. One example of this can be found in a grant UNITE was recently a part of. A major state university was awarded a multiyear federal grant and partnered with UNITE to achieve specific grant objectives. With all three of these entities—the university, the federal government, and UNITE—the timing was complex, because each worked within a different fiscal year. For instance, the grant funds were dispersed based on the federal government's program year, September to August, but the university and UNITE followed their own fiscal years, July to June and August to July, respectively. The variety in fiscal year creates significantly more work for the operational end of the partnering organizations to ensure, despite the calendar differences, that each entity was spending the money appropriately, making all payments, and following the laws and guidelines set forth.

To alleviate these types of complexities that arise when working with multiple partners, try to align your budget timeline in order to streamline operations and avoid confusion. Similar to a marriage, nothing is worse for a relationship between partners than money issues.

. . . for the coordination of resources . . . There are two parts to this segment of our definition, beginning with coordination. Later in the chapter we will discuss how to present the various information needed in budgets, including how the resources will be coordinated and by whom. Many of these details will be presented in the **budget narrative**—a document that accompanies budgets to provide more detailed information. Start considering who might be responsible for paying bills, collecting money, ordering equipment, hiring personnel, and tracking the progress of your program.

The second part of this definition is resources. When most teachers think of grants, they think of funds given to them by another entity used to purchase goods that benefit their students. But grants and, more specifically, the projects they fund, can involve so much more than money. Later in the chapter, you will learn what other resources should factor into your proposal, as well as the nonfinancial ways to achieve your program's objectives.

. . . and expenditures. Finally! In other words, what are you spending your money on? Similar to many teachers, you may have a money management phobia (after all, you didn't become an entrepreneur . . . yet!), but rest assured, this is the easiest part. If you follow the steps within this chapter, you will be rolling in dough and spending it in a responsible manner.

Stakeholders

Before you dive in and write the budget to your proposal, take a moment to consider the various stakeholders involved in this portion of your project.

You. Your role as author and potentially principal investigator (PI) is the most flexible of all roles, because you get to decide who else, if anyone, will take part in the budget. For instance, you may be writing a small, one-time grant to purchase a new reading rug for your classroom. Chances are, in this case, you will work alone and write your own budget, be awarded the money directly, make the purchase yourself, and report how you spent grant dollars. However, a larger grant may compel you to include other staff from your school in the process, such as appointing a budget manager to track money received and spent. Allow yourself the flexibility to play the role best suited for you. If you know you are not the best person to give money to, then bring someone else in. When dealing with money, it is always a good idea to have more people than too few, because it enables more checks and balances.

School personnel. Whether it be a school clerk, administrator, or school board, make sure to get the necessary permissions, gather the relevant information, and complete the correct processes before submitting anything. Each school is different in how it chooses to handle money, accounts, and permissions, so you will need to discuss how funds will be kept, recorded, and accessed with all necessary school personnel. For example, your proposal may include the creation of a new after-school activity. Your administration may want to create a brand-new account just for those funds or may want to include it in a different department's account. Overall, school personnel will be looking to make sure money and resources are being spent in a legal and responsible way. Remember it is the role of an administrator to make sure all activities are in compliance with the laws and mandates specific to schools. There may be rules you are unaware of that could get the school in trouble or even get you fired . . . always check first.

Also, by including more school personnel in your project, you create a positive buzz around you and your project, helping you sustain your project even after grant funding runs out.

One service-learning project ran into a problem when the granting organization restricted the grantee from using funds to purchase agricultural goods. However, the project required three hundred pounds of soil, an agricultural good, to fill school-based garden beds for a healthy eating program. In reading the fine print, the project staff discovered that, although they could not purchase agricultural goods, they could purchase potting soil in quantities of less than three pounds. After discussing their plan with the granting organization's program officer, the project purchased one hundred three-pound bags of potting soil to complete their garden bed restoration.

Granting organizations. You may encounter a variety of stakeholders within a granting organization, but typically, the organization will have a program officer or some other staff member dedicated to the implementation of that particular grant funding. This person is your first point of contact whenever you need to reach the organization. In most organizations, these are staff members who are not included on the selection committee but are there to answer questions related to the RFP, help implement your project, manage money and other resources on the granting organization's side, and report to leadership about the successes and challenges you may be having. No matter your question, program officers are bountiful sources of useful information that could make or break a successful project.

Depending on the structure of the granting organization, you may work with junior or senior leadership at some point. Most foundations, corporations, and nonprofit organizations have a staff and a board of directors. It is the job of the staff to work day to day and produce the goods or services the organization provides. The board of directors guides the organization in its overall direction and most often serves as a financial watchdog to the organization's leadership.

The staff is often led by a chief executive officer, the highest-ranking authority on staff at any organization. He or she is primarily responsible for overseeing all functions of the organization and staff. The CEO answers only to the board of directors who, as an entity, hires or dismisses the CEO. Occasionally, the president of the board and the CEO are the same person. In that case, the board of directors can still vote out an old and elect a new president or CEO based on their own bylaws.

You may be asking, "Why do I care about all of this? I am only going to work with the program officer." or "My grant is for $500 to buy a new book set. Do I really need to know all of this?" *Yes!* First, board members and senior leadership will be looking at how you spend *their* money. They want to know they are getting the best for their dollars and that the money they chose to invest in your project will be well spent. Much of this has to be done in the narrative sections prior to the budget, but a clean budget that matches your narrative is essential in winning a grant. Keep in mind that these people deal with budgets and money all the time and on a much larger scale than your proposal. They are very comfortable and confident in working with financial statements, meaning they should be able to understand your budget quickly and easily. If someone with their level of expertise is left with more questions than answers after looking at your budget, you will probably walk away empty-handed.

The second reason this information matters to you is because of the possibility of relationship. People get involved in foundations and nonprofits not to make money but to create change in the world. It is different from business in that granting organizations' leaders want to care about your story. If you have an opportunity to create a relationship with someone at the nonprofit, seize it.

By developing a relationship with your school, your project, your students, and the leadership or board of directors of an organization, it is more likely they will fund you and perhaps even explore other types of partnerships and support.

Identifying What to Buy

At this point, you have developed your project, identified who should be included, found a funder, checked the RFP for requirements, asked any clarifying questions to a program officer, and have received permission from your school to write the grant. Now, before you start writing your budget, you need to determine what to buy and where to buy it from.

Purchasing supplies. For the purpose of this book, supplies are anything that is not a service, piece(s) of equipment, or personnel. Supplies may be glassware for a new science lab, books for a classroom library, reeds for woodwind instruments, scissors, paper, postage, ink, potting soil, lumber, paint, light bulbs . . . anything. Oftentimes you will purchase supplies in bulk to meet the needs of your project. They are typically low in cost and are needed in larger quantities.

When ordering supplies, make sure to check with the granting organization's rules as well as your school's rules. Oftentimes items used in construction cannot be purchased with grant funds unless you are applying directly for that type of grant. For instance, perhaps your school or state has restrictions on what kind of paint you buy.

> When ordering supplies, make sure to check with the granting organization's rules as well as your school's rules.

Additionally, your school may have rules about how much it can order from one vendor. For example, if you want to purchase paper in bulk from the same vendor your district already uses, you may not be allowed to because your purchase could push the district over a certain dollar limit, requiring a different contract or approval process.

The supply line in a budget is often very flexible. If you are close to the specified dollar limit of the grant and you know a piece of equipment is a set cost, consider reducing the supplies requested or finding them from a different source. For example, if you are starting a new theater program at your school, use the grant dollars to purchase light equipment and either (1) ask the vendor to provide free bulbs for the first order in exchange for a one-year service contract, (2) work with another company to get a good deal on bulbs, or (3) ask your administration, school board, or parent-community group to provide a small amount of money to cover the supplies. Many parent groups and community groups hate to see equipment lying dormant in schools simply because there is no money for supplies (printers but no ink, smartboards but no cables, soccer uniforms but no goals). Use that to your advantage and strengthen your proposal by adding a match commitment (see Matching later).

Purchasing equipment. Equipment is any item that is not immediately consumable. Oftentimes, equipment requires supplies to function and will need some type of maintenance. Sometimes, the line between equipment and supplies is blurry. For instance, although items such as computers, kilns, musical instruments, cameras, and Bunsen burners are clearly equipment, other items such as football pads, physical education equipment, dry-erase boards, desks, chairs, software, and backpacks may or may not be considered the same. Always refer to the RFP when determining what is equipment and what is not. When in doubt, ask a program officer.

When buying equipment, you should make the same considerations as with supplies. Check with the granting organization and school district to ensure you comply with regulations. Furthermore, as mentioned previously, equipment items often need supplies in order to serve their function. A water polo goal needs a pool, water polo balls, swim caps, and players in order to serve its function. Smartboards need a computer, cables, electricity, and a physical location to serve their function. It is this distinction that needs to be highlighted within your grant. Let's say you are writing a Donorschoose.org grant for a document camera. Your budget may look something like this:

Quantity	Description	Product number	Unit cost	Total cost
1	Vidifox document camera	VDC-199547	$359.99	$359.99

Elsewhere in your proposal, you should include language telling the reader that you already have a projector and screen in your room. Perhaps the projector is the only piece of technology in your room and other than bringing in your personal computer, you have nothing else to use with this valuable classroom tool. For a grant like Donorschoose.org, you may have already included that into your project narrative. In other grants, you will include this into a budget narrative where you provide greater detail on your requested line items.

Either way, it is important to remember to clearly indicate your capacity to use and maintain the equipment. A funder would not want to provide you with an expensive piece of equipment only to have it fall into disrepair quickly or for you to lack the supplies to operate it.

Nothing is too small. If you are ordering a new baritone saxophone for your jazz band, mention your existing contract with a local music shop to repair and maintain instruments. If you are requesting a laptop cart, write about where you intend to store it, how it will be charged, who will service the laptops, and what kind of system you will use to check the cart out. Showing evidence of a well-thought plan is always better than leaving readers to assume.

Contractual items. Contractual items are generally composed of the people power included in projects. Services, salaries, and stipends are common line items found in a contractual section of a budget proposal. Most small grants will not include these items, because they tend to be more geared toward supplies or equipment and assume the people power is already provided. However, if you find yourself in need of contractual services, unique considerations must be taken into account, as discussed later in the chapter.

Other items. Most items should fall into one of the preceding three categories. Occasionally, though, items may not fit easily into a classification because of the varying definitions and restrictions created by a funder. A more detailed discussion of some of these issues will be covered further on in the chapter and in the appendixes. For now, let's focus on the purchasing of goods.

Now that you have determined the supplies and equipment you need and have ensured you can indeed purchase it with the granted funds, it is time to shop around. Here are some best practices for shopping around.

- Go to real vendors whom you know and trust. In our Internet-driven world, it is easy to find and purchase products online. It will be tempting to hop online, find your products in a couple minutes, and put them into your proposal. Avoid this temptation, and take the extra time to discuss with others around you what items you intend to include. For instance, perhaps there is an existing relationship that would allow you to get a better price. Maybe a local business will sign onto the project and provide you a larger discount if you are funded.

If you do not have a personal connection to a vendor, make sure to read reviews. Do your research. Nothing is worse than receiving your grant award six months after you submitted your proposal only to find out the vendor went out of business or discontinued your product.

Some granting organizations take out the guesswork for you. Donorschools.org has a preselected list of vendors that you shop directly from, allowing them to control the price of goods, overhead costs, and negotiate for you. Other granting organizations, such as UNITE, ask for a proposal and best estimate but will buy the requested items directly from a vendor, oftentimes saving money and putting more resources into schools when possible.

- Shop around. Just as you would when buying a car, television, or any other major investment, shop around with different vendors. As mentioned previously, some vendors will even provide extra discounts when you explain your projects. If you go with that vendor, make sure to get the deal or discount in writing either in a contract form or a quote.

Your goal should not only be to find the lowest price but also to find the highest-quality product with a reputable vendor. Be flexible in the spending, especially with the supplies line, to ensure you get the best products available.

- Account for all the extras. How much is it to ship this item? Do I need to sign a service contract with this vendor if I buy this equipment? Are there specially designed supplies that I need to buy to get this product to work? All of these are some basic questions you should ask yourself prior to committing to a vendor. Hidden costs and fees can add up and throw a wrench into your well-designed plan.

Another extra can be tax. Each state handles tax differently; some states will not charge sales tax at all and others may. As a school, you should be exempt by the IRS from incurring sales tax; simply show the business your tax-exempt letter (available from your administration) and the vendor should not charge you tax.

Some smaller businesses may not want to accept your tax-exempt status or tell you that they don't participate in that program. This is not true. It is federal law that organizations with this designation be exempt from paying sales tax. You can decide if it is worth your time and effort to explain this to the business owner or simply find another vendor to order through. For more information on tax-exempt status, visit the IRS website at www.irs.gov/Charities-&-Non-Profits.

- Avoid private sales. There is often a delay in time between your grant submission and the award being provided. It could be as short as a couple weeks or as long as a full year. Ordering from a private person can cause problems with price, availability of the product, and reliability down the road.

Private parties often include websites such as eBay, Amazon, and Craigslist. For example, if you intend to request a cozy chair to add to your parent resource room and find the perfect chair on eBay, that chair may be gone when the funding comes. Similarly, businesses like Amazon are able to instantly price their goods in response to market demands as often as they would like to. Perhaps you find that same chair on Amazon, and they have many in stock. The price could potentially change dramatically between submission and award, leaving you to explain the price difference to a funder.

If you must go with a private vendor, get an agreement signed between you and them. Even though this agreement may not stand up in court (not to mention it would cost more in legal fees to get your item at the original cost than it would be to just buy from another vendor at the new cost), it shows the granting organization that you have done your due diligence. It also puts the private party's reputation on the line if they don't follow through with their end of the bargain.

• Make best estimates when appropriate. Some items will be tough to quantify. It may be difficult to determine how much spray paint you need for the basketball court, chalk for the baseball diamond, or glue sticks for a prekindergarten creativity center. Use reasonable estimates in quantities but make sure to have a reliable unit cost.

Budget Prompts

Similar to many portions of your proposal, you may be required to respond to specific prompts in the budget section. Here are four examples of budget prompts for your consideration:

> UNITE has allocated $500 for this project. Proposals can request any amount up to $500. All proposals must include an itemized budget. The budget may allocate UNITE funds up to $500 for purpose of the classroom project only. No funds will be allocated to pay the proposer or any school staff for any time or skills performed during the course of this project. Grant funds cannot be used to reimburse individuals. Goods will be purchased by UNITE on behalf of the winning proposal's school and delivered. Services can be paid through school money, then reimbursed by UNITE. UNITE will not be responsible for paying the state income or federal income tax on any item purchased with UNITE funds due to all parties being tax-free organizations. Include an itemized budget for every aspect of your proposal.

> The program offers two levels of support: general field support grants, which provide up to $50,000 for capital projects not associated specifically with the field surface, including the installation or refurbishment of bleachers, concession stands, lights, and irrigation systems; and field surface grants, which

provide matching grants of up to $200,000 to help finance the resurfacing of a community, middle school, or high school football field and the installation of synthetic sports turf. In addition, a smaller number of matching grants of up to $100,000 are available to help finance the resurfacing of a community, middle school, or high school football field with natural grass or sod. All grant funds must be used for capital expenditures and may not be used to maintain field surfaces.

Let's Play land use grants of $15,000 and $30,000 will support creation of joint-use agreements between local governments and school districts that address cost concerns related to safety, vandalism, maintenance, and liability issues to reopen previously unavailable playgrounds and recreational facilities. The $15,000 grants will support the opening of at least four playgrounds in cities with populations of less than 100,000 people. The $30,000 grants will support the opening of at least eight playgrounds in larger communities. Grants can be used for training and technical assistance, utilities, and other building related to the extra use of the facility, legal fees, contract security services, and marketing campaigns related to the joint-use agreement. Grant recipients must commit to opening the playgrounds within twelve months of the grant decision.

Windy City Youth provides grants ranging from $500 to $5,000 to support innovative programs that engage urban youth in job force development. The majority of proposals funded are at the $2,000 level with very few awardees receiving a full $5,000 grant. Funds may not be used to pay youth, capital expenditures, or indirect costs. Please provide a detailed budget along with a budget narrative describing each expenditure.

Looking at these examples, what sticks out to you? Take a moment and circle key elements of each budget prompt. Let's take a detailed look at each prompt and see if you caught the main points.

UNITE has allocated $500 for this project. Proposals can request any amount up to $500 (*1*). All proposals must include an itemized budget. The budget may allocate UNITE funds up to $500 for purpose of the classroom project only. No funds will be allocated to pay the proposer or any school staff for any time or skills performed during the course of this project (*2*). Grant funds cannot be used to reimburse individuals. Goods will be purchased by UNITE on behalf of the winning proposal's school and delivered. Services can be paid through school money, then reimbursed by UNITE (*3*). UNITE will not be responsible for paying the state income or federal income tax on any item purchased with UNITE funds due to all parties being tax-free organizations. Include an itemized budget for every aspect of your proposal.

1. This grant allows you not only to request a maximum of $500 but also allows you to request any amount up to $500. This useful knowledge indicates to you that this could provide funding for a smaller project and that you do not need to create new expenditures to meet a minimum.

2. This requirement prevents you from paying yourself or any other school colleague. Although it serves as a limitation, it is also an opportunity for you to use your time or a colleague's time later in the proposal as a grant match.

3. Here UNITE describes exactly how the money is spent. This is useful information for a few reasons. First, it alerts you that you must be very detailed in what you want to purchase and from where. Because the organization will be making the purchase, they will probably do some price checks of their own. Second, this eliminates many challenges of handling funds yourself, making it easier for your school to apply for this grant. An administrator will be happy to support you when it doesn't create more work for operational staff. Finally, the prompt specifically mentions that goods will be delivered to your school. This opens an opportunity for you and your school to create a relationship with this funder, potentially leading to more opportunities. Consider having an event or showing your appreciation when the goods are delivered.

> The program offers two levels of support (*1*): general field support grants, which provide up to $50,000 for capital projects not associated specifically with the field surface, including the installation or refurbishment of bleachers, concession stands, lights, and irrigation systems (*2*); and field surface grants, which provide matching grants of up to $200,000 to help finance the resurfacing of a community, middle school, or high school football field and the installation of synthetic sports turf (*3*). In addition, a smaller number of matching grants of up to $100,000 are available to help finance the resurfacing of a community, middle school, or high school football field with natural grass or sod. All grant funds must be used for capital expenditures and may not be used to maintain field surfaces (*4*).

1. You should determine the correct program to apply for.

2. Ensure that you will not be using the funds for these items or apply for the second option.

3. A key word here is *matching grants*. In order to apply for the $200,000 award, you need to have matching funds ready for use. Something to consider. You can also use this to your advantage by bringing this opportunity to a parent group, community organization, or school administration and asking them to fundraise to support this. If they know you can find other dollars, the goal line for reaching the required amount is not as far.

4. A third option is available to you. Also note that you can only use these funds for capital expenditures, which are funds to support a major project, typically construction or the acquisition of a long-term asset. These grants are rare, because capital projects are often very large, complicated, and involve multiple parties.

Let's Play land use grants of $15,000 and $30,000 (*1*) will support creation of joint-use agreements between local governments and school districts that address cost concerns related to safety, vandalism, maintenance, and liability issues to reopen previously unavailable playgrounds and recreational facilities (*2*). The $15,000 grants will support the opening of at least four playgrounds in cities with populations of less than 100,000 people. The $30,000 grants will support the opening of at least eight playgrounds in larger communities. Grants can be used for training and technical assistance, utilities, and other building related to the extra use of the facility, legal fees, contract security services, and marketing campaigns related to the joint-use agreement (*3*). Grant recipients must commit to opening the playgrounds within twelve months of the grant decision (*4*).

---

1. This is different from the UNITE grant in that the funder did not provide a range but two specific dollar amounts.

2. They are very specific on whom you have to partner with and what you will do. This allows you to figure out quickly if you are able to accomplish this project or if it would be too much work to get local government to participate. They also provide you with many buzz words that you will want to incorporate into your proposal and budget narrative.

3. More specifics on what the funds can be used for and what the funder expects from you.

4. The funder provides a very strict timeline, which should be accounted for in your budget, budget narrative, and proposal. Consider adding an action plan to your proposal when you come across time-specific objectives.

Windy City Youth provides grants ranging from $500 to $5,000 to support innovative programs that engage urban youth in job force development. The majority of proposals funded are at the $2,000 level with very few awardees receiving a full $5,000 grant (*1*). Funds may not be used to pay youth, capital expenditures, or indirect costs (*2*). Please provide a detailed budget along with a budget narrative describing each expenditure.

1. Much like the UNITE grant, Windy City Youth also provides a range of funds. However, they go one step further and tell you what a typical grant size is. Always shoot for their suggested size. By starting small, you are more likely to get funded as a new funder. If your project is successful and you are allowed to continue to apply for funding, the organization is more likely to fund larger projects once you have built a history and rapport.

2. Windy City Youth specifies items it cannot pay for. One of those is indirect costs. As discussed previously, indirect costs pay for overhead expenses incurred by an organization. Your school district will be interested in knowing this, because they may require indirect costs at a predetermined rate for incoming funds at certain levels.

Budget Presentation

Chances are, as a teacher, you will be applying for smaller grants (under $2,000) the majority of the time. If you have never written a grant before, it is better to start there and gain some experience before moving on to larger grants. In this section, you will learn how to create and present a budget to support a small program.

> More advanced budget presentations and examples of all kinds of budgets are available later in the chapter and in appendix A.

Use their outline. Many organizations who work with schools and teachers know that creating a budget from scratch can be a barrier to getting high-quality candidates. You will probably encounter a funder that provides a budget format for you to complete in lieu of creating one from scratch.

Always use these forms. This also simplifies your life creating more time for you to write more grants! Also, reviewers will be looking closely at your proposal, and submitting your own or changing the provided form will create more questions than answers.

Be careful of these dangers when using a provided form:

- **Misplacing items.** Make sure that all of your supplies are listed in supplies, equipment in equipment, and so on. They provide you a format to ease the budget-review process, not complicate it. Your requests need to be clearly categorized into the provided columns and rows. Avoid creating a disorganized shopping list.

- **Check your math.** Assuming the form is a paper form and not an online program where you input information (such as Donorschoose.org), triple check your math. Create your own version in spreadsheet software first, and allow the program to do the math for you.

- **Complete it last.** You may realize you forgot to account for space rental, gasoline, or other supplies that will make your project work. By completing your budget last, the form will be well organized, preventing you from reprinting and correcting budgets.

- **When in doubt, ask a program officer.** Perhaps there is not a column or quantity, or there are not enough lines for you to list everything you intend to purchase. Instead of trying to create a solution that you hope they will understand, call a program officer and ask for his or her advice. If that officer tells you to add your own budget or adjust their form, make sure to reference that clearly on your application by stating what adjustments were made, why you made them, and the program officer's name who advised you to do so. This will ensure you will not lose points off your application.

There will be many organizations that do not provide you with an exact format, form, or guidelines on what to include. The following is a short list of core items that should be on every budget.

> Be mindful of application requirements, because some grantors do not want you to provide any kind of identifying features to ensure a fair evaluation. Always follow their directions.

Identifying features. This may include your name, school name, project name, application number, or any other identifying item that will match your proposal to your budget. Adding these features to your budget in an easily visible location will help reviewers who may have separated your proposal and are reviewing hundreds of applicants.

Quantity. This is your first column on the left of the page. How many of that specific line item will you purchase? Make sure to match this number with the program narrative. It would be highly suspect if you are running a painting program and choose not to order much paint.

Description. This column should be shown immediately to the right of quantity and provides a brief description of what it is you are purchasing. Context is important when discussing how much detail you should provide in this brief mention. If you are only asking for $300 for a new dry-erase board, consider listing "24′ × 4′ Acme dry-erase board" instead of simply "dry-erase board." If you are requesting many different items, such as $2,000 worth of musical instrument supplies, it may be too much information to be that detailed. In that case consider listing "Vandoren clarinet reeds" instead of "Vandoren Pro-line 2, 2.5, 3, 3.5, and 4 sized clarinet reeds." Be efficient, clear, and precise. If you find that you need more space to explain, simply include more detail in the budget narrative.

Product number. This column will be to the immediate right of description. Information such as product number may not be needed depending on your project, but it can be useful to some funders. When ordering from a smaller organization, an organization that will purchase items for you, or when requesting very specific items, include this number to ease the process of price checking, procurement, and delivery. This is also a handy way to free up space in your description. You can create a simple explanation but provide a product number allowing funders to search out exactly what it is you want.

Unit cost. To the right of product number (or the description, if you are omitting product number) comes the unit cost. How much does each item cost individually? This should be without tax, shipping, or any add-ons. Depending on the size of your grant, you may not want to include cents and change into your costs. If you are buying a product that is $356.78, simply round up to $357. A good rule of thumb is to round up on all proposals unless otherwise stated.

Total cost (line). The final column appears just after the unit cost, including a total cost. This should simply be the quantity multiplied by the unit cost. Again, do not include tax, shipping, or other add-ons.

Shipping. Include any cost of freight and shipping. Make sure to use conservative estimates and not simply the lowest cost possible because shipping rates can change. This should not be shown as a separate column but as a line item within those columns, as if you were purchasing shipping. Specifically, as written across the budget, the shipping should be presented with no quantity with a simple description such as "ground shipping," no unit cost, and a total cost. It should also include the total amount required to ship all products. If your project requires the purchase of stamps or other shipping needs, that should not be included here; it should be a separate line item. This shipping cost is only the costs associated with shipping the goods indicated in the budget.

Total cost (project). At the end of your budget, a total cost including all of the line items and shipping costs should appear on the lower, right side. It should be aligned with the total cost of each line. This figure is oftentimes bolded or underlined.

Take a moment to sketch out a format using these columns. Once you have created all of your columns, fill in as many rows as needed. After completing all of your expenditures, leave a blank row, then include shipping. Add another blank row, then compute your total cost.

Compare your sketch budget to this. How did you do?

Quantity	Description	Product number	Unit cost	Total cost
1	Vidifox gooseneck document camera	VF-243654B	$ 300	$ 300
2	Sony USB connecting cables	46599846	$ 17	$ 34
1	Acme power strip		$ 16	$ 16
	Ground shipping			$ 20
	Total cost			$ 370

Here are some real examples of simple budgets. The formatting has not been changed from their submission to highlight the importance of a structure in your budgets. As you review them, recall the list of items and general formatting rules previously outlined. Take some notes on elements you find appealing and elements that could use some work. Try and view them not only through the eyes of a grant writer but also through the eyes of a funder. How does this affect the list of items you wrote down?

Example 1

> **Budget:**
> Transportation = $200
> Supplies for the project = $100
> Supplies to promote awareness (fliers, posters, pamphlets, mailings) = $200

Example 2

DESCRIPTION	QTY	Unit Price	Total Price
M0912E BLANK UNLINED 9" x 12" Dry Erase Board Review Item	4	$2.60	$10.40
MC0912 BLANK UNLINED 9" x 12" 30 Student Combo - includes 30 Dry Erase Boards, 30 Dry Erase Markers and 30 Erasers Review Item	2	$108.00	$216.00
DEM - Item Code Student Dry Erase Markers 36 Pack Purple Review Item	1	$25.20	$25.20
Total			$251.60
Coupon			
Shipping U.S.A.		$25.16	$276.76
Grand Total			$276.76

Example 3

Budget

Item	Price per item	# of item	Price
Elastomeric paint (5 gallons)	$118.00	2	$236.00
Striping tape (180 feet/roll)	$20.77	5	$103.85
Bean bags (set of 8)	$15.95	4	$63.80
Playground balls (set of 6)	$27.95	1	$27.95
AcceleRope speed ropes (set of 6)	$17.95	2	$35.90
NFHS baseballs	$3.95 each	8	$31.60
			Total: $499.10

*No additional charges for the following items:

- Measuring tape, which will be provided at no additional cost
- Power washer to clean concrete prior to painting will be provided at no additional cost.

*Prices taken from the following sources:

- www.gophersport.com
- www.homedepot.com

Take the list you just made and compare it with ours. What items did you catch that we did not? Do some items conflict? Which ones are in agreement?

Example 1

- This was submitted as it looks. Just a quick block of text under the narrative section. Although the numbers are simple, it still lacks presentation, giving the impression that it was done quickly.
- The specific items were very vague. Even though the project's need statement may explain how you intend to spend the money, always be detailed in budget. For example, is the $200 for transportation for a bus, train tickets, or gas reimbursement?
- Instead of saying "supplies to promote awareness" and listing a few items, those items should be listed as separate line items for this small of a grant. How many fliers do you intend to make? Are you paying for postage? If so, how much and why not use a cheaper alternative such as e-mail?

Example 2

- This was also submitted as it looks. The advantage of copying and pasting an online shopping cart is that it makes the writing process quicker and easier for you. The disadvantage is that it sticks out in a bad way to the reader and once again shows that you may have not taken the time to author this yourself. Not only is this visually distracting but it also includes elements not needed such as "review item" and "coupon." Plainly stated, this looks unprofessional.

- The reviewers of this proposal commented that the teacher may be able to get better prices on the dry-erase markers and erasers by purchasing in bulk instead of a "student set." Remember that the grantor will typically know the field and items associated with your grant. Practice due diligence in shopping around.

Example 3

- This example follows formatting procedures: a clear, left-justified title, subtitles for each column, and an itemized listing of products.

- The author should have used the word "Quantity" instead of "# of item." When possible, spell out words instead of using symbols.

- The notes at the end are a strong element to this proposal. The RFP did not call for a budget narrative, so the author snuck in important information that the grantor might be wondering at the end. Not only does it show that they made an effort to find matching resources but also that they have thought through their project and will not be scrambling in the eleventh hour to find a measuring tape or pressure washer.

Final Tips: The Simple Budget

We hope you have gleaned some good ideas on how to create a simple budget for your proposal. When in doubt, remember these few tips:

- Keep it simple. Stick to the major headings, and make the budget easy for your grantor to read.

- Formatting goes a long way. It is not difficult to build a table in a word processor or copy and paste from a spreadsheet program. Take the extra couple of minutes to present your budget in a professional manner.

- Whenever allowed, send all of your grant items, especially the budget, in a PDF format. This will enable your formatting to remain consistent each time someone opens or prints your document.

- Do not overspend. Even if you plan to cover the costs with your own money, do not overspend the budget. Instead, highlight in-kind or in-cash matches (more detail later in the chapter).
- Get assistance when you need it. It is better you submit a well-crafted budget that someone helped you with than to do it yourself and submit something that will leave a reviewer with questions. Ask your administrator, mentor, and even family member to take a look to get their opinion.

Advanced Budget Techniques

Imagine you are hurrying into school, three bags under one arm holding a coffee precariously in the other hand, trying to sign in for the day minutes before the first bell rings. Your principal sees you walking in, and despite your best attempt at dodging eye contact, she catches your eye . . . and she has you.

"Good morning! Didn't you just pick up that new grant-writing book?"

"Yes . . . ," you manage to squeak out trying still not to spill your precious coffee.

"Great. I came across this wonderful grant opportunity to help us start small learning communities here in the school. I am really slammed with work [a lie . . . we all know it], so do you think you could take a stab at it?"

Once you are labeled a successful grant writer, that new title will stick with you everywhere. Suddenly teachers and administrators will be asking for your help on their projects or simply to take another one of your own. Eventually, you will bump into a larger grant that may require a few more items than the items in a simple budget.

This next section is designed to be a quick crash course in some of the more common advanced budgeting techniques to get you started on a more complex project. Keep in mind that we will be focusing again on how to create and present a budget with advanced elements inside. The topic of money management is one many other books cover.

Some larger grants may include the items that follow. Some of these may not be specifically mentioned but will often be found in more advanced proposals, so it is good to have a basic understanding of them.

"The Cost of Doing Business"

There are some items that you may have to include to simply make your project work. Here is a quick list of items for you to consider and suggestions on how to account for them in your proposal.

Sales tax. When we say sales tax, we include any tax attached to the procurement of a good or service. Common examples are state sales tax on goods purchased through a merchandiser, hotel taxes for hotel rooms, and environmental taxes for the procurement or disposal of certain materials. First and foremost, check with local and state laws regarding your tax code. Some states do not charge sales tax and others charge only for service industries. As a school, you are exempt from federal tax and usually, by extension, state sales tax. That often does not extend to certain types of tax, such as hotel tax.

You do not necessarily need to include tax directly into a line of your budget, especially when working with large figures. Instead, make sure you account for the after-tax amount in the request. For example, if you are including travel expenses to attend training on small learning communities, factor the tax of airfare and lodging into the cost of those two line items.

Due to loopholes in our current (2013) tax system, many online retailers do not charge tax if they are shipping goods out of state. When possible, quote online retailers for goods and compare to a local provider.

If you are unsure of the exact tax dollar amount, find the general tax rate for the particular state and add it to your line item. Best-case scenario, you overrepresent that particular line item and end up saving the grant money by being under budget.

Shipping. Although we have already discussed shipping, it is worth mentioning again in the context of a larger grant. It would be excessive to include shipping into a large grant budget, especially if you are dealing with multiple purchases over multiple years. In some cases, it is beneficial to have a line item specifically for shipping costs, especially if you plan on sending and receiving many parcels. In other cases, shipping may be wrapped into the line item and not specifically mentioned.

Make this judgment call based on the overall presentation of your budget. When in doubt, simply call the program officer and ask if he or she wants it included or not.

Copying, postage, and other consumables. When working on larger grants, it may not make sense to articulate exactly how much paper you will need. For example, if you are writing a grant to start an extension of your school's special education services that will serve students with autism, then trying to determine exactly how much paper you will need is probably not possible. Same could be said for postage, pens, pencils, and other consumables used during the usual and daily operations of your project.

There are a couple of different methods you can use to associate cost to those items:

- Most people simply take their best guess. They will treat this money as "filler" and throw it in as an afterthought. However, this is not the preferred method of accounting for consumable needs because it has many pitfalls. What if you underbudget and find yourself mid–school year with no copy paper left? What if you overbudget and your proposal gets thrown out because your budget is off? Avoid this method at all costs.

- Ratios. Take a moment to figure out how many pens or paper your whole school uses in one year. Divide that amount by the number of people in your building who use paper (don't forget office staff, community groups, and others who have access to school resources). Then apply that figure to your expected staff number for your new program. Last, add in any additional need you may expect over the average. You could also apply the number of students in place of the number of users to account for student-specific usage of a material. Here's the equation:

  School paper use/number of users × number of users included in proposal = total requested amount (plus any additional need)

- Research similar programs. When developing larger programs, it is typically best to follow a model that has been tested. This enables you to learn from others' successes and shortcomings and get the most out of your new venture.

We hope you have developed a relationship with another institution that is already implementing a similar project. Go beyond just asking about their programmatic structure and ask detailed budgeting questions. You may be surprised to hear some valuable suggestions from colleagues. Use of pens, paper, and postage may not be riveting conversation, but it sure can make your life a lot easier and provide a concrete basis for your request.

Hiring People

Personnel can be a very tricky part of grant writing. If you are working on a proposal that involves bringing new people on board or simply providing more funds for current workers, make sure to take into consideration these few steps:

- Do not assume you can hire people. School districts in particular have extensive human resource rules and regulations set in place. Many grants have been written and awarded only to find out they cannot perform a major function of their project simply because there is no way to hire people.

- ○ Check with your human resources office, administrator, or school board to determine the exact processes. This would be a conversation you want to have early on before you invest hours into writing a proposal.

- Be thorough. Is the new employee a full-time or part-time employee? If he is part-time, does he receive benefits? How about full-time? Is she a union member? Does an official human resources designation exist for the work that person will be performing?

  - ○ These basic questions should start this conversation with officials at your school, but a mock-up of a draft job description is also a useful tool in this conversation, because oftentimes designations come down to the work being performed.

- Explore all possibilities. Is there another option? Can you provide a stipend to someone? Is there a partnering organization willing to hire that person for you? Is there a professional service you can hire out?

  - ○ Nonprofits are your friends here. There are many nonprofits around the country doing great work and looking for new projects with money attached. Sometimes, you may be able to split a position with a partnering organization, giving you a part-time worker and the organization a part-time employee. That arrangement also allows your school simply to cut a check to the nonprofit and let the organization deal with all of the implications of hiring someone.

- Factor in all of the costs. If you are going ahead with hiring someone, include all of the costs associated. Benefits, FICA, and unemployment tax are just a few items to consider. Simply listing the base salary will not cover your costs.

- Consider the extras. What is the cost of background checks? Will this person need a desk, chair, office, or other resources that you do not already have? If you are hiring the person as an independent contractor and providing a stipend, do you want to include a buffer amount for the tax the person will have to pay come April 15?

The best advice when considering hiring people is to go to the people who know best—those who hire for your school district. This can be a very complicated process, but it is one well worth it. If you can find a way to do programmed recess, start an after-school program, or provide in-school tutors using grant dollars, you are providing a very rich experience for your students. Make sure to follow the rules outlined by your district, state, and funder, and you should be fine.

Indirect Costs

Indirect costs are fees included into your proposal by your own school district or partner organizations for the cost of managing the grant. This is how many nonprofits and some school districts fund or offset the cost of administrative staff, office space, and utility bills. These costs are usually expressed in a preset percentage that should be attached to your final subtotal. See the following partial budget example.

	Abbreviated example	
Project subtotal	$13,589	
Indirect cost at 7.5%	$1,019	
TOTAL AMOUNT		$14,608

Indirect costs can be a sticking point for major funders. If you are working with multiple partners, you run the risk of incurring large indirect costs from each partner, limiting the amount of money that goes directly to the project. Some organizations' indirect percentages are also very high (20 to 30 percent), which can deter some funders. Here are some techniques to combat that:

- Check with the grantor to see if they have a set limit or set percentage rate that should be applied. The federal government is very good at setting low indirect costs as requirements for obtaining grants, forcing organizations to lower their cost to get funds.

- Use it as a bargaining tool. If you are partnering with an organization and the organization has a high indirect cost, you can target that first in negotiations to increase the amount of funds directed to project activities. Keep in mind, indirect costs support the project indirectly (thus the name). You can make a strong case for a smaller percentage, especially if the partner is heavily invested in the project.

- Consider managing the grant yourself. If a partner organization is going to charge a 20 percent indirect fee for grant management, make the case that you and your school staff will manage the majority of the grant. The organization may bring its amount down if you have clear roles specified for each partner. Plus, by managing the grant yourself, you are bringing more indirect funding to your own organization.

- Convince your school and partners to provide their indirect cost as a match to the grant. This is a great way to allocate funds to the project without actually spending money or resources directly on the project. Read the following detailed section on matching.

 For more information on advanced budgets, as well as examples, see the appendixes.

Matching

Matching is the allocation of funds (in cash) or resources (in kind) to a project that offsets the cost of the proposal. This section will outline the two major types of matching, demonstrate how to present a match in a budget proposal, provide common types of matches that can be used to support your project, and discuss the processes required to secure a match from partners.

A match shows funders three things:

- That you are serious about completing this project and have already dedicated time, energy, and resources into its development

- That the financial burden is not placed solely on their funding

- That your match, especially in multiyear grants, will demonstrate how you plan on sustaining your work once grant funds are used up

As mentioned, some RFPs may require a match. This is usually expressed in a percentage of the total amount received. For example, if you are requesting $100,000 from a federal grant, you may be required to match 25 percent (or $25,000) in cash or in kind. Other grants may not require or even mention a match in their RFP. Demonstrating a match commitment, though, can go a long way in showing your dedication to this project.

In-Cash Matches

The first kind of match is an in-cash match. This is simply as it sounds—a cash amount already dedicated to your project. You can procure in-cash matches in a number of ways. For one, you may already have funds allocated from a school budget line that will go to supporting this project, or perhaps another organization will promise to provide funds when you are awarded the grant you are working on. Whatever the source, there are a couple of items to consider:

- Make sure the in-cash amount is reasonable in your overall project. Although some may say that no amount is too small, an in-cash match of $100 in a $300,000 grant may not be worth presenting in your proposal. You can still use that match, but do not feel pressured to incorporate disproportionate amounts in your budget.

- The cash must be real! The best kind of in-cash contribution to put in a proposal is one that you already have. The next best option is promised money with documentation (see later in the chapter). You cannot count items such as "anticipated donations" or "projected ticket sales." If a grant is asking for specific information on how you will meet the match, stick to real cash. If the RFP is general and asks you only to commit to meeting a match, items like those just listed will work, because you do not need to account for them in your proposal. Check the RFP or with a program officer for details.

- When accepting cash donations from other organizations, ensure that they are organizations your grantor would want to be in business with. Small details such as foundations restricting matching gifts from other foundations can lead to a snag into your plans. For instance, when applying for federal funds, you cannot use other federal funds as a match. In another scenario, if you are applying to a grant through an environmental organization and one of your partners was recently in the news for creating havoc in the environment, you may rethink your partnership with them.

In-Kind Matches

In a typical grant, the majority of the match requirement will come from in-kind matches. An in-kind match is any noncash resource used during the operation of your project. These items can vary from individuals' time to the use of equipment or space within an existing building. Often, there are very stringent requirements on what will count as an in-kind match and what will not. Here are some general guidelines to get you started:

- When using someone's time as an in-kind match, ensure that you use an appropriate rate. For example, if you hold a meeting with a partner and the grant does not pay for that partner's salary, you can allocate the time spent in the meeting on your match report. Take the duration of the meeting and multiply it by the partner's hourly rate. (You may need to figure out the hourly rate from the partner's salary. Contact the partner's budget manager to see if there is a predetermined rate to use because oftentimes "consulting rates" do not actually make up the "hourly rate.")

- If you use a building space and your grant is not covering any cost associated with that space (including rental fees, utilities, rent), you can count that as a match. The manager of that space will either need to provide you with a quote of how much he or she would usually charge an outside group to use that space or a cost breakdown of how much per square foot it costs to operate that space.

- Make sure to get accurate documentation. Simply saying an organization provided $5,000 of in-kind services is not enough. Have sign-in sheets at meetings. Get invoices that indicate the amount of services rendered with a zero balance showing it was donated. Keep accurate monthly or quarterly logs of in-kind contributions.

- Push other members of your team to find in-kind donations and report them. The task of reporting in-kind matches is often pushed aside until the year or grant end when you need to report back to your granting organization. Stay ahead of the game by having team members report back to you regularly.

Fourth-Period Review Guide

✎ A budget is a plan for the coordination of resources and expenditures.

✎ Five best practices when shopping for goods or services are as follows:
  - Go to real vendors that you know and trust.
  - Shop around.
  - Account for all the extras.
  - Avoid private sales.
  - Make best estimates when appropriate.

✎ Read grant prompts carefully and adhere to their requirements.

✎ A simple budget presentation should show the following:
  - Quantity
  - Description
  - Product number
  - Unit cost
  - Total cost

✎ Never overspend your budget!

Fourth-Period Exit Ticket

1. Who are the stakeholders interested in your budget and why do they matter?

2. Which of the following would *not* be considered an in-kind match?

   a. A volunteer's time working on your project

   b. Donated space for an event

   c. The use of equipment that was not purchased by the grant

   d. A skilled worker's labor for which you paid for with grant funds

   e. None of the above

Fifth Period: Personal Finance

Take a moment and Google the phrase "teacher misuses money" or "teacher arrested for misusing money." There are loads of articles out in the press of teachers and other school officials "stealing" money from the school. Although some of these teachers may be guilty and are indeed taking money, others might not even know that they have been "stealing."

That being said, this short chapter is meant to keep you out of jail; we don't want you to be in that second category (and we assume you're not in the first). It does not matter how big or small the grant is, once there is money involved, you must be careful of how you manage those funds.

This is not a comprehensive discussion on accounting or fiduciary duties or a replacement for a CPA or school clerk. Instead, this chapter is intended to equip you with survival skills needed to protect yourself. Always seek the advice of qualified and certified members of the financial services division of your school when dealing with matters of money management.

Pay Day!

Congrats! You won the grant you have been working on for weeks. That $10,000 is sure going to come in handy in running your Model UN program for students. Now that you have the money, though, what do you do with it?

First, recall the discussion in chapter 4. Some grants may not give you the actual funds; they may spend it for you. This is great news! You don't have to worry about a thing and can skip right over this chapter!

However, perhaps the granting organization does give you the money. They may dispense it all at once or they may give it out in installments. Some grants will require you to invoice them for the funds, adding a layer to the budgeting needed to implement this award. However they decide to give you the money, you must follow a few rules to keep you, your school, and your relationship with the funder safe.

Who Will Be the Fiscal Agent?

Figure out early on who will hold the money. This doesn't mean who will literally hold the physical cash, but, instead, who will be the bookkeeper for these funds. How are the funds stored and in which accounts? Your school administration and clerks may already have a solution for this, but it is important for you as the grant writer and principal investigator to be involved in this process. Here are a few examples:

• *The large pot approach.* Some schools may choose to stick the funds into a large pot of money. In the accounting world, many accounts are limited to their uses (furniture accounts can only buy furniture, capital funds can only be used in capital projects). You will hear a lot of this when schools discuss firing teachers. They may have funds locked up in another account that cannot be transferred to fund salaries.

There may be an account that your funds can go into that has little restriction. The benefit to this approach is that it is fairly simple for your administration to see and use that money, and it does not require the creation of new accounts. The downside is that it is more likely your funds could get spent on other items.

If this is the approach you take, make sure to keep your own journal on deposits and expenses. Routinely check your notes with the clerk to ensure your money is still there.

Ask questions, get clarification, and, most of all, remain part of the accounting process.

• *The department approach.* If you are in a departmentalized school, you may already have a department budget. The clerk may have a line or a series of lines intended strictly for your department into which you can deposit these funds.

This allows you to keep a closer eye on the funds and ensure they are being spent in the appropriate way. A drawback is the added responsibility put on you and possibly a department chair, adding another person to the mix.

• *The dedicated account approach.* Many teachers who are familiar with grants prefer this route. Your school clerk or administration would create a separate account where this money would live. No other funds would go in, and only approved project-related costs would go out. This allows for extreme control and transparency in how funds are spent.

The downside to this approach is, once again, the extra responsibility placed on you. If you are the only one with access to the funds and something goes wrong, the line points clearly back to you.

Whichever way you choose to hold the money, make sure all of the details are covered among you, the clerk or accountant, and school administrator. Clerks and accountants do this every day, so they may be tempted to dismiss you quickly, but persist. Ask questions, get clarification, and, most of all, remain part of the accounting process. Think of it this way: you wouldn't give your paycheck over to a friend to spend on your behalf each month.

Getting Intimate with the Numbers

If your project is a small project in which there will only be one expenditure of cash, and all of the money will be spent at once or the money will be handled by the granting organization, you can stop here. However, if that is not the case, the following are helpful hints on how to track and manage the spending of grant funds.

Granting organizations may disperse money in a variety of ways. Some organizations may give you the entire amount all at once and others may require you to invoice them as expenses are incurred. Both methods require a level of fiscal responsibility that goes beyond the usual call of a teacher.

First, make sure to keep an accurate log, or a ledger, of each deposit and expense. This ledger may look very similar to your checkbook at home and can be easily tracked in spreadsheet software. For example, when a granting organization disperses funds to you, either at the start of a project or through an invoice your school submits to it, you can record that as a "credit" to your account ledger. Once you begin spending those funds, "debit" them from the ledger. Keep in mind that this is an account that may exist on paper only. When we talk about accounts, it does not have to mean that your money is in a dedicated account. Instead, you are tracking the money that is specific to your project.

Here is an example of what this might look like: You have received a grant to start a robotics club. The grant will provide $20,000 that can be used toward building materials, travel money to attend competitions, and a small stipend for a coach. On the first day of school, September 1, the granting organization provides you with $5,000, enough to get started and show that you are using the money correctly. You

Keep your own log, even if your clerk is keeping track. Having two ledgers is a key element in financial reporting.

If you are an accountant who happens to be reading your husband's teaching book, across this book, we are using credit and debit in the basic sense and treating all accounts as cash accounts.

make the order the next day and purchase $2,350 in supplies. What would your first two ledger entries look like?

Cash in Robotics Grant Account

Date	Description	Credit	Debit	Balance
				$0
9/1	First installment	$5,000		$5,000.00
9/2	Robotics Inc. – supplies		$2,350	$2,650.00

Simple, right? You can expand this simple template to include more categories as well, which will help you classify and describe each transaction. For example, instead of just one "description" category, you may want to add "vendor," "purpose," "check number," or "summary" to give you a higher level of organization and detail. Do whatever makes the most sense to you. Ideally, you will be the only one reading your books. When it comes time to report, you can process the information and display it in a much more user-friendly way.

Did you notice how we recorded the purchase of supplies when we made, not received, the order? Make sure to always record transactions at the time they occur, not when they are realized. For example, your school may order those goods on a credit card and then pay the credit card bill with the funds for the grant. This is a completely legal method of using the money. Imagine, though, that you were not keeping books or did not record the transaction at the time it occurred and waited until you received the goods. Your ledger would still read "$5,000," which could lead you to think you have more money than you actually do.

More likely, your clerk who is keeping his or her own record of your account might tell you that you have more money than you actually do on September 25, because the credit bill is not due until September 30. You may end up overspending your account. Keeping an accurate record and marking transactions when they occur will prevent most of these issues from happening.

Double Check

Make it a habit to check your books with your clerk's every now and then. It is important for two people to have independent books and then compare them for inaccuracies or mistakes.

If you do not have a clerk or another person to keep a dual record independent of yours, enlist the help of a parent, colleague, or school board member. Try

One school district recently uncovered a small accounting mistake that made the district appear to make $16 million more than they actually did! Although that is no small figure, the mistake was a small one; they credited the wrong year for the mistake.

We hope you will not make a mistake that amounts to a $16 million mishap (if so, I suggest you read about a good law defense rather than this grant-writing book!), but small mistakes can do a lot of damage, too.

your best not to have someone who supervises you directly keep a dual record, because it could lead to problems later. It is easy to pass receipts on to a third party with a good communication plan.

Security

In the accounting profession, practices to create consistency and reliability from company to company are called the generally accepted accounting principles (GAAP). They are enforced by various government agencies, and although each country may have a different method, there is movement to have international consistency in these same principles. In an ideal world, these practices would prevent situations such as what happened with Enron, WorldCom, and the $16-million mistake made by the school district. There is no need to know all of the principles included in the GAAP; however, the security of money is vital in demonstrating your reliability to your administration and external grantors. Certain security precautions can be made in order to maintain trust and transparency in how you handle grant funds.

Your school district may already have many of these controls in place. If this is the case, your next step is to have a thorough discussion about your role in those. In the event your district does not have such stringent controls, you can implement many of these controls yourself. Once again, you are dealing with other people's money and, as such, have a much higher level of scrutiny. Do not take these items for granted; implementing some of these easy steps could not only save you a huge headache down the road, but may also save your job.

Here are a few internal controls that would be easy for you to implement:

• *Establishment of responsibility.* The premise of this internal control is to designate or restrict individuals to specific roles within financial transactions. Your district most likely implements this already by granting access to some individuals to pay bills and granting access to others to create invoices. If you are working with a small district or are required to complete all of the financial transactions on your own, ask for a volunteer to assist you, and establish duties between the two of you. Perhaps one of you collects and counts money and the other person records the amount after double checking the count. Another example might be that one individual places orders with vendors and the other pays the vendor.

Most important, if a grant allows extra pay that will go to you, never sign your own paycheck. Internal controls help prevent someone from stealing money. Signing your own paycheck, even if legitimately, looks highly suspicious.

- *Segregation of duties.* Different individuals should be responsible for related financial activities. Have you tried to order something through your school before? Were you able to just call up the vendor, use a school credit card, and purchase your goods? If there are effective internal controls, you should not have been able to do that. One of the most important controls that could be implemented is segregation of duties.

If the previously described scenario had implemented a segregation of duties control, it would look like this: You wish to order some supplies through a selected vendor. You choose what you want and send your order to someone inside the school or district for approval. They approve the purchase and send it off to be purchased by a purchasing agent. A record of those goods is recorded with the purchasing office and the person who first authorized your order after you receive them.

The key difference from the first one here is that it would be nearly impossible for someone to create factious orders or invoices or pay a company that benefits themselves.

Here is another example: You plan on using your grant funds to buy tee shirts for a schoolwide event. Your brother-in-law owns a shirt-printing company and offers you a heavily discounted rate if you bring business to him.

Now if you were able to make the order, pay the order, and receive the goods without any approvals, you can see clearly how an outsider (maybe a rival company that usually prints shirts for the school) could make a conflict of interest claim against you. A better method to avoid this would be to involve an internal third party, such as an administrator or clerk. You can provide this internal third party with the quote from your brother-in-law, as well as other quotes you have found. They may wish to do their own searching as well. Once they have determined that it is indeed in the best interest of the school to go with your brother-in-law's business, they can place the order and allow you to receive the goods. The advantage is obvious. The disadvantage is that it will take more time by involving more people, but the trade-off is worth it.

The second major consideration under segregation of duties is that the record keeper and the person in physical custody of the item should not be the same person. Another way to put this is that someone other than the person working with the products should independently keep a record of the items purchased.

Here's an example: You have won a restorative justice grant that permits you to start a DJ club after school. Being the leader of this grant, you purchase DJ equipment for youth to use in your club. Because you purchased it, there is no direct record of the equipment other than your own. Do you see the issue? What prevents you from taking that DJ equipment home with you and making it a permanent fixture in your house? Having another person record the purchase of that asset prevents you from taking custody of the product.

This idea can get tricky when it comes to smaller grants such as Donorschoose.org. Because those grants purchase the items for you, you must be clear with the funder whether the items are yours or the school's.

One good example of this can be seen in a university program that goes to great lengths to parse out these nuances. In this university's teacher induction program, each new teacher and mentor receive one piece of technology. If they successfully complete the program, that piece of technology is theirs to keep, as long as it remains a classroom tool. In the event that someone does not complete the program, that piece of technology is forfeited to the school where the teacher works, not the university. However, if a teacher transfers from one school to the other but still works in the serviceable area of the mentoring program, that technology will follow the teacher.

Make sure you know who owns your equipment, and, whenever possible, have an independent person record the acquisition of those items.

- *Documentation procedures.* Documentation makes everyone feel a lot better about where and how money is spent, so document everything. Keep receipts. Match them up with invoices, shipping slips, and bank and credit card records. When dealing with actual cash, have it counted by multiple people and ask each to sign next to his or her name after counting it. Keep records of check numbers, dates, and any other information that will help you keep track of transactions.

Make and keep copies of all checks, invoices, packing slips, and other related

If the items purchased do not belong to the school but are awarded directly to you, consider employing this same internal control by having the items added to your homeowner's or renter's insurance policy. Another option is to get clear language from the grantor as to whom the items legally belong. Always plan for the worst-case scenario.

documents. You can stay organized with a filing system or binder that is separated by type of document or in a chronological sequence. Try to avoid having one overstuffed file folder for your entire grant. Consider having your clerk or other record keeper initial or sign key documents including checks. This will certify that they, too, acknowledge the receipt of the document and have recorded it appropriately.

Finally, get signatures whenever possible. When having items shipped to your school, request that the shipping company have someone sign for the package. Many schools have fallen victim to "missing shipments" of goods only to find out that another person in the school accepted the package and thought it was supposed to be used for something else. In some school districts, packages have to go through a centralized distribution center operated by the district. Having packages signed helps you track your shipment as it leaves the world of bar code tracking and enters the abyss of school storage rooms.

- *Physical controls.* These controls have to do with the physical security of various assets. Whether you are working with cash or products that you have purchased, think carefully how you intend to keep those items safe. Is there a locked storage room for those new basketballs you ordered? How about a locked cabinet to store the new tablets? Accepting cash at an art show? Do you have a lockable cash box and a locked location to store that cash box after?

There are many ways to answer these questions and secure your products and goods. Make sure to take in consideration not only the physical control but also the access to that physical control. Many banks have drop boxes where they deposit money throughout that day. Only certain members of the bank have access to those drop boxes, preventing theft.

If you lack certain physical controls or spaces that would aid in the protection of your goods, see if you can work it into your budget request. Oftentimes when ordering items, you can order related items, such as storage bins, racks, and cabinets to secure your belongings. Funders would be happy to help you make their investment a long-term one by preventing theft.

The sad reality is that theft typically happens when someone has access and opportunity. Although we all want to trust our colleagues and students, it is best to eliminate access and opportunity, thus lowering the temptation of theft.

Here are some methods to reduce opportunity and access ultimately leading to good physical control:

○ When possible, keep items (such as cash and small but valuable goods) out of sight and locked up. At the surface this may be obvious but try to be mindful of who sees you putting away materials. It would be best if fewer people knew where you kept certain items.

○ Use tagging. Many institutions tag or otherwise mark their materials clearly so that they are easily identifiable. Stickers, bar codes, quick response (QR) codes, and serial numbers are a few easy ways to mark property and prevent someone from stealing an item.

○ Keep up-to-date and accurate records of all serial numbers, bar codes, and other information in a safe place *away* from where the materials are stored. Keeping the binder with the equipment information in the same unlocked cabinet with all the equipment is a recipe for disaster. Perhaps you can keep your records in the school office or in a colleague's workspace.

○ Take photos of your materials. Oftentimes, photos help in documenting the existence of a product in the event it is stolen. Insurance companies may ask for photos to not only prove you indeed did have the product but also to provide information on the quality of the product, which can come into play when making reimbursements for loss.

○ Create a checkout system or logbook. If you are working with small electronics, large machines, musical instruments, books, or any other material that individuals will be using, it is always best to keep a logbook tying the user to the equipment. One common mistake is not related to theft but to damage to traveling laptop computers stored on carts. As they are passed from classroom to classroom, undoubtedly computers will break or be vandalized in some manner. However, many teachers do not have a logbook of which computer was assigned to which student, making it impossible to effectively correct the misbehavior.

• *Independent internal verification.* This last consideration was partially addressed already. By keeping your own ledger and records, you allow yourself the opportunity to verify your records with the other independent party in your school. Periodically, check your records against theirs. If there are discrepancies (beyond transposition issues or typos), take the records to the next level of management to help sort it out. Although you would most likely be able to solve the issue between the two of you, having a third party involved protects everyone from accusations of bad accounting and money mismanagement.

You can see now why it would be desirable to have the person keeping the dual record to yours be someone who does not directly supervise you. If your records reveal an error on his or her records and that person is your administrator, it could create a tense situation and put you in the middle of an ethical dilemma. Try and have a school clerk, parent, or school board member fill that role.

Reporting

The final function of good money management is reporting. Chapter 7 provides follow-up procedures although an attempt to address financial reporting is made here to realize the whole process.

Companies and nonprofits, both large and small, are required to submit financial reports periodically. Largely, these reports are used by lenders, owners of companies, board members in nonprofits, and other crucial parties that use these reports to decide if they should continue to buy a company's stock, donate to a nonprofit, or, in our case, continue to fund your project.

Financial reporting is an effective method of generating new support as well as maintaining current financial support from grantors. Once again, this conversation lends itself to larger grants in which more than one expenditure occurs.

Checkpoint

Many grantors may have reporting requirements already in place for your grant. Government grants in particular require a high level of reporting, with foundations a close second. If you already have to report to your funder, make sure to use their formats and paperwork. If your grant does not require reporting or the reporting is not substantive, here are a few easy steps that create a high-quality reporting system.

Timeline. Just as you created a timeline for your project, decide with your team what your reporting timeline should be. It could be as simple as once a year, at the end of the project, or once a quarter. If your grant is very active with lots of funds going back and forth, it may be wise to create quarterly reports. Another way to look at quarterly reporting is if you are trying to raise a match or donation amount to sustain your project. Quarterly reporting can take the form of progress monitoring and encourage future donations.

Similarly, it may be wise to simply report at the end of the project or year. For example, if your grant supports a transition program to aid freshmen students' transition into high school, it may be wise to report at the end of the year so you can highlight the academic progress of students along with the financial operations.

As mentioned in chapter 4, remember to consider the various fiscal calendars when constructing your reporting timeline. If your fiscal year is different from your funder's, it may affect when reports take place. For example, you may need to send out reports for the closing of the fiscal year even though your project is only halfway done. Perhaps you then choose to report twice a year so as to avoid creating more work for yourself.

What to report. Financial reporting, in the context of grants, largely consists of informing readers of two financial functions: revenue and expenses. The report should include any income that you have received on this specific grant project and any expenses you have paid. People want to see how money is coming in and how money is being spent.

Financial data alone will create more questions in the minds of your readers than you want. It is vital to tell a story with your numbers. As you report revenues and expenses, make sure to report progress-monitoring data as they pertain to your project.

> Financial data alone will create more questions in the minds of your readers than you want.

For example, if you are implementing a grant that provides professional development for teachers, a report would include how much money you have received, how much money you have spent, how the money gets spent, and how much money is left. Following this, you would want to discuss how many teachers have been trained, how many students have benefited from this training, how students increased their test scores as a result of the training, and other metrics you are including in your evaluation plan (see chapter 7 for more details).

When choosing what to report, try to keep in mind the reasons you are reporting in the first place. You not only want to keep those intimate with the project informed of your progress, but you are also informing the public at large of your success.

How to report. There are a number of effective methods of producing effective financial reports. Most companies use a standard format, consisting of four major reports: the balance sheet, income statement, statement of owner's equity, and statement of cash flows. You can adjust this method to meet your needs by using two of these reports: an income statement and balance sheet. Between these two reports, a reader can learn where your money is coming from, how much money you have spent, how much money you still owe, and what other assets you have.

For many teachers, the balance sheet and income statement are too cumbersome and time consuming. Plus, you should not be dealing with additional debt or equity holding of your grant project. Instead, you may choose to take the "nonprofit" approach.

The nonprofit approach is a preferable format to mimic, because it strikes the balance we are looking for between effective reporting and effective promotion. You have probably seen reports provided by nonprofits that show how much money they have, where that money has come from, and how they have spent it. They often incorporate this with progress-monitoring data and language that articulates their future plans.

Play around with a number of techniques. Try to incorporate some graphs into the mix. For example, if you have multiple revenue sources, use a pie chart to show how much money has come from each source. You can use that similar technique with expenditures. We have included in appendix B a few examples of nonprofit reports that can be imitated in style and purpose.

How to disseminate. Now that your report has been written, edited, and been approved by the people who need to approve those items, it is time to disseminate the information. First, meet the requirements set forth by your grant. If you are required to send your granting agency a report, send it to them first. Always meet their demands first.

After meeting your contractual obligation, you may want to send this report in the sense of a follow-up to administrators, colleagues, and the general public. Other methods of dissemination include sending it to a school's website or local news sources, creating a press release for local media outlets, sending a flier home, creating e-mail blasts, or posting on social networking sites. If you do not have someone who can contact the media on your behalf, consider writing your own press release and sending it along; most news agencies have a general e-mail address you can send it to. However, be sure to ensure that permissions, such as those pertaining to your freedom to release student data or use images of youth, are met before sending anything out.

In general, give this report to everyone possible. Hand it out to students, and ask for their input. Have extra copies in the front office and teachers' lounge for teachers and parents to pick up and read. Send it home with students. Provide it to community and parent groups, even if they are not involved with the grant this time.

Fifth-Period Review Guide

- While writing the grant proposal, determine who or what entity will be the fiscal agent, that is, who will control the money.
- Keep an accurate log or ledger of all incoming and outgoing funds.
- Ensure that a trusted, independent person is also keeping a logbook to avoid errors, abuse, and questions regarding fraud.
- The five types of security are as follows:
  - Establishment of responsibility
  - Segregation of duties
  - Documentation procedures
  - Physical controls
  - Independent internal verification
- Make a habit of reporting financial information to the public on a regular basis.

Fifth-Period Exit Ticket

1. Define the "dedicated account approach" to money management.

2. Read the following scenario and answer the following questions:

> Ms. Espinoza at Griffin Academy has been awarded a grant to create a peace room in her school. This room will be used for students who need an alternative space to focus themselves before returning to class and will be left open all day available to anyone. A teacher or other school staff member will staff the room during prep periods on a rotating schedule.
>
> Ms. Espinoza and her clerk have decided to keep dual books of all financial activities including the purchasing and receipt of new furniture and small board games for the space. They will meet once a month to compare ledgers and correct any mistakes. Ms. Espinoza chooses the items she wants to buy, brings the information to her clerk, who then gets administration approval to put the items on the school credit card. When the goods arrive, both Ms. Espinoza and the clerk keep a signed copy of the receipt and packing slip for their records.

a. Which of the five controls are missing?

b. What are some steps you would take to add the missing control?

Sixth Period: Statistics

"Students, standardized test scores increased by 12 percent on completion of the project."

"Attendance increased from 87 percent to 95 percent over the term of the project."

"Students demonstrated a deeper understanding of the material with 76 percent receiving mastery-level scores compared to only 54 percent in the control group."

Data collection, analysis, and presentation are vital components of any grant project. Without data, it is substantially more difficult to prove that a grant-funded project made the impact the writer intended. As a teacher, you probably already understood this. You know that progress-monitoring data, standardized test scores, and data-based decision making have made a significant comeback into modern classrooms. More and more often, teachers are required to collect various metrics to assess their students; some districts even spend up to fourteen full instructional days on testing over the course of the year.

Whether or not you agree with the importance placed on data in the classroom, there is no argument that the use of statistics can enhance, and in some cases make or break, your project proposal. Your statistics are often your connection to the world. Throughout this book, we have reminded you to take the readers into consideration. The public at large responds to data, and it is no wonder that the business leaders who operate many of the nation's grant-making organizations are data-driven leaders.

This chapter will guide you through the basics of using statistics to support your proposal, creating an assessment plan for your project, implementing that plan, reporting the results, and avoiding the common pitfalls that grant writers make when working with data.

 People have made entire careers of working in education statistics and data collection. This chapter is meant to serve as a rough guide and cannot replace the valuable knowledge from a skilled professional. Collaboration is greatly encouraged.

Using Statistics to Support Your Proposal

In our data-driven world, statistics are essential elements in providing a solid justification for a grant proposal. The use of statistics can either make or break a proposal by either offering too little data-supported information to justify your project or by offering statistics that are unrelated to your projects. Here are a few guidelines for you to follow as you research and include data into your proposal:

- *Do your research.* There is a study out there for everything! Be sure that, when you find your data, it comes from a reputable source and is confirmed by other studies. Additionally, citing research from a rival entity is never wise. Try to learn the political landscape of the funding and research community by reading articles, responses, and seeing past-funded projects to determine what kind of statistics should not be included.

- *Include relevant information.* The information you include in your proposal should meet at least one of the following criteria:
  - It provides essential context for a funder to understand my project.
  - It provides logical reasoning and justification for my proposed project.
  - It is the exact metrics my project seeks to address.

A common mistake is the inclusion of demographic data as an indicator of need. One project submitted to a funder included the following statement under the student's needs section:

> Our students are 98 percent African American and 2 percent
> Latino and come from many single-parent households.

Never mind the poor grammar or the lack of a much-needed frequency or ratio for the "single-parent households" comment; this author is using demographic data to articulate need. A student's ethnic, racial, gender, religious, and so on breakdown *does not* indicate need. Certainly these facts and figures can be useful when providing context relevant to the project, but unless there is a clear, logical connection to the grant purpose, it is irrelevant.

- *Know your audience.* Some granting organizations will be very interested in research and will want to know if your proposal is rooted in proven findings or accepted practices. In other cases, the overuse of data can come off as pretentious and overbearing, turning off some funders. Whenever possible, try to connect with past awardees and see a sample of their proposal. Another option would be to take a close look at the RFP and get the sense if a funder would require lots of data to back up your project.

- *Cite your data correctly.* Choose a citation format and stick to it. Some grant proposals come out looking like a dissertation and others sound like a conversation between colleagues. Both are acceptable and have a place in the grant world, but be sure to give credit where credit is due in both instances. If you feel that using APA, MLA, or footnotes would be too obtrusive or cumbersome, make sure to work the citation into the narrative.

Statistics can be added into almost all portions of your grant proposal, as long as they follow the described guidelines. Regardless of the size of the grant or funder, it is always best as a professional educator to base your decisions on research. Show that in your proposal, when appropriate, and your likelihood of being funded will grow.

What Is the Purpose of Assessment in Your Project?

Assessment is the only method in which to prove the effectiveness and success of your project. Although you may feel that a project has made a significant impact on your target audience, you must be able to measure it in order to truly understand the degree of success or failure. There are other compelling reasons to create, implement, and report your assessment plan that can be best explained by viewing the assessment needs through various stakeholders' perspectives.

You

The very first person concerned with whether or not your project was successful is you! An effective evaluation not only allows you to determine if your proposed project was a success, but also provides valuable insight into the creation of future projects. As you become a seasoned grant writer, you will want to continue to learn from past projects. Keeping accurate records of your assessment plans enables you to build from project to project, increasing your likelihood of receiving future funds and also making you a stronger educator.

Additionally, administrators and colleagues are very interested in your project and can benefit from your assessments. For example, let's say you were awarded a grant that allowed you to purchase and use a frictionless track for your physics classroom. Because of this, perhaps your data on student understanding of force is significantly higher than that of a colleague's across the hall. That colleague would be very interested in learning how you used the technology to create a better understanding of the material and try to replicate it. Your administration might even be pleased with your results and choose to purchase frictionless tracks for the entire physics department.

Your Funder

Your funder will want to know if you have met the goals and objectives you stated in your proposal. When a granting organization provides resources to you, they are making an investment in the goals you stated in your proposal, not just you and your students. Funders want to know if their investment has paid off.

Funders also report this philanthropic activity as progress toward their overall goals. The Boeing Foundation is able to include strides taken in science education through its charitable giving. Your data provide the basis for their existence and, in some cases, their ability to secure more funds for future projects. The same applies for the National Endowment for the Arts (NEA). If your project provides more dance instruction to youth and young adults, the NEA is able to count your project's results to their own progress in reaching their goals and objectives.

External Users

School boards, parents, community groups, and other funders may not be looking for your data, but I bet they would be interested! By reporting the success of your project in a data-based manner, other groups affiliated with the school are able to stake claim to the gains made, instilling a sense of pride in your school. You may also attract positive attention to your programs, creating more opportunities for projects and funding. Often forgotten, this group can prove to be valuable when presented to. Just because they don't ask doesn't mean they are not interested. Share your reports widely, especially if they are successful!

Overall Process

The assessment process breaks down to five steps:

1. Create an assessment plan.
2. Collect data.

3. Adjust the project according to your data (if applicable).

4. Analyze the data.

5. Report the findings.

As an educator, this process is somewhat familiar to you. Think back to the last lesson or unit you taught. Did you go through a similar process to determine how you would grade or assess the understanding of your students? Did you take a moment during the middle of the unit to adjust your lessons or schedule based on the scores students were receiving mid-unit? Afterward, did you take a deep look at your assessment data to determine if your unit or lesson was successful? Did you talk with your students or colleagues about it? The process you work through with your lessons is the same approach you should take with grant assessment.

Check out this example of a kindergarten music teacher's unit on "keeping a steady beat." Note to yourself which stages of the assessment process each action addresses.

Starting on Monday, my twenty-five kindergarten students will begin a week-long unit on "keeping a steady beat." This skill is often taught at this age and is in line with national standards. My overall plan is to complete a preassessment by having students march to the beat of a song and noting how many students are able to keep the beat in their feet. During the week, we will continue to explore movement through gross motor skills at varying tempos with the primary goal of keeping a beat. On Friday, I will play the same song as I did during the preassessment and note how many students are able to keep the beat in their feet.

On Monday, I noticed only twelve of my students were able to consistently march steadily to the beat with the selected song. On Tuesday and Wednesday we worked with new songs and continued to march. I noted, however, that many students were able to much more effectively pat the beat on their legs while sitting than they were when marching. On Friday, I conducted two final assessments using the song from Monday. First, students were asked to march to the beat. Then I replayed the song and asked students to sit and pat on their legs to the beat. When marching, nineteen students were able to keep a steady beat while marching. However, while sitting, twenty-two students were able to keep the beat effectively.

On the following Monday we discussed as a class if it was easier keeping a beat in our feet or in our hands. I discussed my assessment with a colleague familiar with early childhood brain development and learned that gross motor skills are being acquired during this age and there is great variance in ability from student to student. When talking with the kindergarten classroom teacher, he informed me that his class is very active and that he routinely has them sitting down when they are required to focus.

Although you may not write out a lesson or unit reflection in this manner, you probably go through this same type of thought process. Did you notice how similar it is to our grant-writing assessment process? First, the teacher created the unit plan and then collected initial data. A mid-week analysis of the data revealed that a better strategy might be emerging and adjustments were made to the instruction and assessment plan to accommodate these data. Final data were collected, and on analyzing, the data showed an improvement in many students, though not all students were reached. In reporting to the various colleagues, the music teacher learned valuable insight into what made this unit successful with some and not with others.

The classroom example demonstrates that, as a teacher, you already know how to build these plans! Couldn't this example be an excerpt from a report to a granting organization? If the teacher was using grants procured through the National Endowment for the Arts with the objective of providing music education to students in the early grades, this activity is a clear and measurable outcome of the project's success.

Many of your grant proposals will somehow be linked to student achievement. By thinking through your grant as you would a lesson or unit plan, you will have already developed the skeleton of an assessment plan.

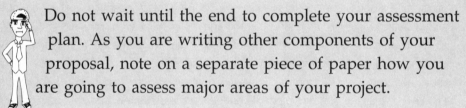

Do not wait until the end to complete your assessment plan. As you are writing other components of your proposal, note on a separate piece of paper how you are going to assess major areas of your project.

Step 1: Building an Assessment

How does this assessment plan differ from your lesson? What if your project is not directly tied to instruction? To help you answer this, go back to the RFP (the granting organization's mission and vision statement is useful here, too) and answer the following questions:

- *What specific outcomes is the grant looking for and how am I meeting those outcomes?* Although it may seem basic, ensure that your assessment matches not only what the RFP is asking, but also what your project is proposing. Many projects are thrown out because their assessment plans did not match the project's intent or the project description. This is often a by-product of waiting until the very end and rushing your assessment plan.

- *What data are currently available in the topics the RFP is addressing?* Regional trends make a great deal of difference when finding which data to measure.

Research what kind of data is being collected on your topic, and decide to follow suit or go against the grain. For example, would you want to report on ACT or SAT scores? Would you prefer to use a widely accepted behavior management data collection measure or develop your own method of measuring behavior in your school? Depending on the funder, location of the funder, and type of project you are applying for, these decisions change.

- *Am I meeting all of the requirements?* Some RFPs can get very lengthy. Double check to ensure you are assessing everything that needs to be measured.

- *Am I measuring too much?* If you are writing a $1,000 grant for a new copy machine, do you need to measure the reading scores of your student body? Probably not. Make sure the work matches the reward.

- *Is this data useful to this granting organization or to my project?* It may be tempting to "pad the stats" by including assessments that you know are going to look positive, but remind yourself that these data are not valuable to you or the funder. Many funders want to see progress or growth in their selected fields. You will want to use the data to make future decisions and determine if you are going down the right path or not. By asking yourself if the data in question are important enough to include in an annual report or presentation to the school board, you can help decide if your data plan is high quality.

Qualitative versus Quantitative . . . That Is the Question

Quantitative data are measures of values or counts and are expressed as numbers. Qualitative data are measures of types and can be represented by a name, symbol, or number code. To put it more simply, quantitative data deal with numbers that can be measured, whereas qualitative data deal with descriptions that can be observed but not directly measured.

EXAMPLE

Quantitative: A class of thirty-one students has an attendance rate of 98 percent. Of those thirty-one students, 76 percent of the students receive free or reduced lunch.

Qualitative: Students in the classroom have brown, black, and red hair. Students receive As, Bs, and Cs on quizzes.

A high-quality assessment plan combines the use of qualitative and quantitative measures. Using a blend of these two general types of data enables a reviewer to understand the whole picture.

For example, when submitting a proposal for the creation of a student government association at a local middle school, the grant writer is able to include a variety of measures to ensure reviewers see the entire impact. They could include quantitative data such as the following:

- Increased school attendance rate among participants
- Increased grade point average among participants
- Percentage of the entire student body engaged with the project
- Number of projects initiated by the student government association

Qualitative data may include the following:

- Increased confidence of students involved in the project
- Increased student participation in other school activities
- Growth of leadership skills among participants
- Increased perceptions of belonging and pride in the school

Although quantitative data is more concrete, and therefore easier to assemble, qualitative data can also be collected in meaningful ways. There are many methods to capture and indirectly measure qualitative data. Many tools, surveys, measures, and other scales are available publicly that allow researchers to assess the growth of observable dispositions such as those just described.

No matter which kind of data you work with, they are used to test an effective measure. It would be best to work with a researcher who specializes in these fields to help develop your methodology when assessing qualitative data. If one is not available at your school, check with your parent organizations or community organizations in your area.

Another source of researchers ready to assist can be found in colleges and universities. Faculty members are often excited to be involved in school-based projects and are connected to the research world. Partnering with a faculty member may even lead to conference presentations, publishing, and further funding.

The vast majority of grants available to teachers will not require elaborate assessment plans that need the assistance of an outside professional. It is still valuable to include qualitative and quantitative data in your assessment plan, even if you are not measuring something as ambiguous as school pride.

In most cases, successful teachers use quantitative data to *measure* their project and qualitative-esque data to *tell* the story. Here is one teacher's example from a recently funded project involving yoga in the classroom:

> On implementing the yoga curriculum daily, student referrals for disciplinary action fell sharply from seven students per week to two students per week. Many students reported feeling "calm" and "in control" just weeks after the program began. This change in atmosphere was also accounted for in the decrease of student conflicts outside the classroom resulting in a 46 percent reduction in target students' time spent in detention. Additionally, students commented it was "easier to focus" during class resulting in a 22 percent increase on course assessments. One student reported "Having yoga at the start of my class gives me a break from the day. It's like a check-in place where I can get rid of everything that happened before class."

In this example, you can see that the teacher did not *measure* the qualitative data pieces but still included quotes that mention categorical data (emotions, feelings, perceptions) without quantifying it. Pairing those pieces of the story with quantitative data that were formally collected provides a reader with the complete picture.

Type of Data to Collect

Much of the data you already collect as a teacher can be used in your proposals. The following list provides some ideas of common data collected and reported on grants:

- Attendance rates
- Quantity of participants
- Test scores
- Grades
- Graduation rates
- Retention rates
- Growth on academic standards
- Number of parents and community members involved
- Performance-based measures
- Resources provided per pupil

Step 2: Collect Your Data

Once you have a solid plan and begin implementing your project, you should begin to collect your progress monitoring data. Collecting your data should be as simple as completing the steps indicated in your stated plan, but often, this is where fatal errors occur. Whether you are using surveys, completing interviews, reviewing test scores, or comparing attendance rates, be mindful not to fall into common pitfalls.

- *Stay on schedule.* Many awardees fall behind on their data plan because they are too busy implementing the program. Make rules for yourself to ensure you will collect the data. For example, if using surveys, make a rule that you must start the program with the survey before doing anything else. Include data collection into your lesson planning if applicable or appoint someone responsible to remind you to collect data. Many data points are time sensitive and cannot be done at a later time.

- *Stick to your plan.* You may find that your data are not showing the results you anticipated. Perhaps your project appears not to be working. Although you can often add data measures to capture the whole picture midway through a project, you must always complete what was approved by your granting organization. It is not unreasonable to think you may not have included everything needed in your assessment plan at the beginning and want to change items during the project, *but* you were awarded your grant in part because of your assessment plan. To change the plan would be to change the project, something funders do not tolerate. If adding items, it is always best to check with a program officer at your granting organization and ensure that your measures do not require a baseline measurement at the start of the project.

- *Keep it legal.* There are many laws and policies that protect individuals, especially children, from potentially harmful research. Many schools have institutional review boards or research review boards that ensure all research and data collection is in accordance with the law and the professional standards that exist in the research community. Student grades and test scores are often very confidential and may have to be treated anonymously. Know your school's policy on research as well as any state laws that may apply before collecting or sharing data.

- *Get permission.* Oftentimes, people must consent to research and have the option to opt out. This becomes even more important when minors are involved, because parent permissions are often a key component of the legality of data collection. Check with your administration to determine if you require special permission for data collection or not. Although you may not need permission to collect grades in your own classroom, you may need it for collecting grades in other classes or reporting grades to the public.

> Keeping information anonymous is usually acceptable in reporting standards. When creating your plan and collecting your data, determine if it is possible to lump your data together to talk about a class or school as a whole instead of individual students.

There are many methods of collecting data, some of which will be natural to you as an educator and others that may require additional research. Following are some categories in which data can be found. Within each category, there are suggested methods you can use to collect data. Please note that this is not a comprehensive list. It is always best to work with a qualified professional or larger group when deciding your methodology.

Academics

Many funders are now looking for stronger ties to the academic success of your students and your proposed project. Whether you are writing a small grant for textbooks or a larger grant for a service-learning program, you may want to consider measuring the academic growth of your students.

> A common signal to reviewers that an applicant is new or inexperienced with data is the attempt to prove causation. Very rarely would your program actually *cause* a result. Instead, your results may show significant correlation—that is, statistically significant results—to the implemented project. Be mindful when writing your proposal and reporting your results to avoid making causal statements if you cannot back them up.

Many of these methods should be fairly familiar to you. You could, for instance, wish to measure the change in test scores associated with a project or use some other academic achievement measurement to highlight the growth as it relates to your proposal. Other academic measurements can be tied to national standards or a teacher effectiveness framework, such as the Danielson Framework for Teaching.

Take a moment to list out how you currently measure your students' academic success. Limit yourself to the five most common methods you use on a regular basis. Keep in mind, you will need routine access to these data, so national or statewide assessments with long timelines may not be the best choice.

1. _____
   _____
2. _____
   _____
3. _____
   _____
4. _____
   _____
5. _____
   _____

Now, using a project of your own or using the project in the following, convert all five of your assessments into measurable outcomes that you would include in your grant proposal. One has been provided for you as an example:

Grant prompt: You are writing to secure funding for new software that will enable you to create more meaningful and student-specific connections to your content area.

Example statement: Students will increase their word-per-minute scores by 25 percent during the course of the project as measured through pre- and post-DIBBELS assessments.

1. _____
   _____
2. _____
   _____
3. _____
   _____
4. _____
   _____
5. _____
   _____

Check out the appendixes for more examples of assessment plans!

Schoolwide Information

Your proposal may be best suited for schoolwide data. Some examples are attendance rates, attendance at parent-teacher conferences, enrollment figures, teacher involvement, aggregate academic growth, and anything else that would affect the entire school population. As previously mentioned, use discretion when using these metrics, because your project needs to match your assessment. For example, if your project benefits only the third grade, you might not want to include overall attendance. Instead, use only the third grade as a point of measurement.

Culture and Climate

Many large school districts have created assessments to measure a school's culture and climate. These measurements can cover everything from a student's sense of safety to the school's healthy food options. This emerging trend is on the minds of many philanthropic organizations and could create support for your proposal. Ask yourself a few basic questions to see if your project could include culture and climate measurements:

- Would my project create a safer space for students to grow?
- Does my project address behavior issues in my school?
- As a result of my project, would I expect to observe a lower referral rate for disciplinary action?
- Am I creating a college- or career-focused environment that can be measured through retention rates or some other related metric?
- Are my students completing homework on a more regular basis or turning in more assignments on time?
- Has bullying in my classroom decreased?
- Do students view our school as a safe, fun, supportive, enriching, and worthwhile place to be?

There are many tried-and-true measurements that exist to evaluate these questions. Usually, these topics are measured through the use of surveying, a common data collection technique. Take a few moments to research surveys that provide insight into these topics.

Whenever possible, use a vetted survey instrument instead of designing your own. Many people spend their professional careers developing, testing, and proving the effectiveness of their surveys or scales and make them publicly available for use. Using one of these certified instruments strengthens the validity of your data. If you are curious and want to dabble in making a survey or are using a small grant and don't intend to make correlation and causation statements related to your project, there is a survey template in appendix A using a five-point Likert scale. Be careful, though, in passing off your own surveys as valid instruments. Check with a program officer to determine the level of reporting needed.

Parent Engagement

Parents can be a key stakeholder in any grant project, and they should not be ignored as a potential source of data during the assessment phase. There are many ways to measure parent involvement in the school, including attendance at parent-teacher conferences, attendance at schoolwide events, time spent with their children on school-related activities, and participation in governance of a grant-funded project.

Community Engagement

We have deliberately separated the parents and the community within this book. Too often, parents and community are lumped together, creating a narrower worldview for the school. Instead, the community and its many resources should be viewed as a separate entity, rich with opportunities that would benefit your school.

Community involvement can be measured in a number of ways. There are many attendance metrics, such as attendance at meetings, school events, community events, and project-related events that provide useful information to the funder. Additionally, you can rate the school's involvement in the community through measurements, such as the number of community events completed, the number of nonparents involved in school and project governance, the population of students involved in out-of-school activities, and so on.

This is also a great area to bring back those culture and climate measurements. Did your students' perception of their community become more favorable? Have your students become exposed to more community-based jobs? Are students more civically engaged than before? Get creative when including the community, because it can add a great deal of substance to your project.

Step 3: Adjust the Project According to Your Data (If Applicable)

Your project may provide you with an opportunity to adjust at some point during implementation based on data you have been collecting. Of course, this largely depends on what kind of project you are completing, what the timeline for the project is, and if making a change is allowable and feasible.

Take a look at these examples and determine if an adjustment could be made to improve the results. If so, what would you suggest that adjustment be?

> **1.** You have written and been awarded a grant that allows you to make a one-time purchase of ten new computers for an aging computer lab. In your proposal, your assessment plan indicated that "students' test scores on statewide assessments

will increase 7 percent in the first year across subjects" and that "community engagement will increase in our school by serving no fewer than one hundred community members in after-school job readiness trainings offered through a local partner organization."

Answer: No, an adjustment is unable to be made based on midterm data. Certainly, you can collect midterm data over the course of the year to determine if you are meeting your goals. You can even make adjustments to try to meet those goals, but unless the funder plans to take back the new computers if the goals are unmet, there is no reason (speaking strictly from the funding side) to adjust your project. Of course, the funder would hope you would adjust your use of the computers if indeed you were not meeting the goal, but, at the end of the day, an adjustment is not required by the funder because the purchasing was a one-time deal.

2. You have been asked to coauthor a one-year grant creating a partnership between your school and three others in the district. This grant would provide teacher training on classroom management strategies, fund stipends for two teachers in each building to conduct observations, and provide money for substitute teachers, allowing grade levels to meet at a common time. The funds will be doled out by quarterly invoices from your school to the funder. Along with the invoice, the funder requests progress-monitoring data to ensure the project is on task.

After the first quarter, you (having been put in charge of the data collection after reading this book) realize that your attendance from partner schools is below the quarterly projection by 15 percent and that referrals for discipline are at the same levels as the year prior.

Answer: Yes! You can and must collect interim data with this project. In fact, the funder requires it of you in order to receive your stipends. What modifications, then, can you make to the project? Should you withhold money to partner schools until their attendance is at the level it should be or is there another way? Do you think the teachers have had enough time to incorporate the new techniques into their classrooms yet or is it too early, causing an identical first-quarter referral figure as last year? What would you do?

Here is a final note on making adjustments to your program. You should never make a change that will dramatically alter the project from what was originally proposed, even if you never have to provide follow-up data to the funder. Funders make their decision based on your initial proposal and to dramatically change it would be unethical and potentially damaging when under consideration for future opportunities. When in doubt, check with a program officer before making any changes to ensure they are allowable.

Step 4: Analyze Your Data

At the end of your project, you will most likely be swimming in raw data. Now comes the time to analyze your data and determine if your project has indeed created the impact you articulated in your plan.

Important: This book will not provide a how-to approach on data analysis. Entire volumes are dedicated and available on this topic alone. You are encouraged to explore this topic in detail by taking a course at a local college or reading up on the subject. If you are in need of detailed methods of analysis, consider consulting with a professional in the field who would be able to donate some time and effort to your project. This would also create a great in-kind match for your project!

Remember that many of these items are already available to you as a teacher. Certainly your school has attendance and grade records. You may be collecting data for statewide assessments or interim testing already. Many times, these sources analyze the data for you and provide those results that can be copied over into a report.

If this is a foreign field to you, start simply by calculating items such as mean, median, and mode. Standard deviation and variance could provide a deeper look into your raw data, followed by regression analysis. Once again, if these concepts are unfamiliar to you, consult with a professional or explore the topics through the numerous online tutorials and available literature.

Step 5: Report the Findings

As mentioned at the beginning of the chapter, there are many stakeholders who will have interest in your results. You, your funder, and external users all have unique needs when it comes to reporting your findings.

Your needs. You may want to determine not only what succeeded and failed but also which elements specifically worked well and which items did not. You will most likely be just as curious about the minutia of your project as you are about the big-picture results.

Your funder. Your funder is primarily interested in if you have met the goals and objectives you outlined in your proposal and if you stayed on course with your project. Depending on your project's size, this could be very general, so adding additional evidence could help tell a deeper story. However, it is always best to report to funders exactly what they ask for, and then have additional research and reports ready if they ask for those.

External users. Depending on the audience, external users fall somewhere between your needs and your funder's needs. If an external user is a school administrator, he or she may be more interested in some of the gritty details, whereas a visiting school administrator, district official, or potential future funder may only require the broad strokes.

Let's look at an example and see what information you may want to report for each category:

> You have been awarded a $7,000 grant to implement the national Girls on the Run program in your school. In your proposal, you discussed that the program would recruit fifty female students to participate, that the school attendance rate of participants would increase, and that participants' self-esteem would rise in a statistically significant manner.
>
> At the end of the program, you find that you were only able to recruit twenty participants instead of the fifty you desired. Additionally, the attendance rate of the twenty participants neither increased nor decreased in a significant way. However, participants' self-esteem did positively and significantly increase.

What information would you report to whom? What additional questions would you want answered, looking through the lens of each stakeholder category?

You. Although you already know the overall outcomes, you would be very curious to learn more about the minutia of the program that caused your findings to be what they are. For example, why was it difficult to recruit fifty girls? Is the age range too restrictive? Is the time commitment too much? Are there so many other activities going on that yours simply wasn't attractive enough? Perhaps adding a survey of the entire target population (third- through eighth-grade girls) or asking questions about their knowledge, assumptions, and level of attraction to the program would answer those questions.

Also, why didn't the attendance rate increase? Did your school have an attendance issue before (i.e., was it a realistic goal)? Did the twenty students who did participate consist of the most dedicated students in the school? Was there no incentive to attend school in connection with the program?

You should know the answers to these questions because they relate to your project. You may never put it in a presentation format, but they will certainly be nagging at you and be on the minds of those in your building.

Your funder. First and foremost, funders will be interested in the results in comparison with your stated goals. A funder may or may not be interested in why you were unable to get more students or why the attendance rate did not increase. However, most funders would be very interested in what happened with their money!

Did you miss that? In your proposal you were awarded $7,000 to support fifty students. However, during your project, you only worked with twenty. Did you end up spending the appropriate 40 percent ($2,800) or did you spend the entire amount? What is your justification for that amount? Why were funds not reserved for future use or returned to the organization?

It is vital to get into the shoes of your funders. Of course they will be very happy that twenty young women received services, but they will be curious as to how you spent the rest of the money and that you were unable to spread the most good. When creating your report to funders, take a moment to either ask yourself questions as if you were the funder or ask a friend to play devil's advocate for you.

External users. In addition to the overall findings, an external user might be interested in what it would take to replicate this activity at another location, grow this activity at your school, or sustain it for future use. The external user may want to see how it connects to other school-related activities (academic areas or after-school programs) and what other services are similar to it in the area.

This is also the time to pull out the really positive portions of your findings and incorporate them into public documents. In this example, you may want to post the findings on increased self-esteem in a school newsletter, website, or other publicly accessible venue. Because you have more information available, it is ethical to highlight some of your achievements along with a short description of the program, provided you extend an opportunity to receive more information if a reader were interested.

Here are some other best practices to take into account when reporting your data:

- *Have additional reports ready.* Having some reports that outline broad strokes and having others that get into the details will save you time and frustration in the long run. Oftentimes, it is best to complete a detailed report and then pull from that one report to create multiple documents able to be sent to various audiences.

- *Always have more research ready.* When it comes to evaluation, it is never a good policy to do the bare minimum. If your project specifies completing only three or four assessments, be sure to add additional measures along the way. Don't forget about the value of qualitative data as a supplement to the hard numbers.

- *Transparency is welcomed.* Remember your ethical guidelines—the ones you bestow on your students daily. Some of your data may not show you the results you wanted. Although you do not have to advertise the shortcomings of a project, you can include those results in a report with an explanation of what went wrong, what adjustments will be made in the future, and other commentary that may be appropriate. It is always best to create a sense of transparency when it comes to the results of projects and the success or failure of an investment.

- *Be prepared to take recommendations.* Many stakeholders may want to add their two cents about your results, conclusions, and future projects. It is best policy to accept these with open arms, even if you have heard the same piece of advice thirty times before! By accepting feedback from stakeholders, you strengthen your relationship and, additionally, their likelihood of future support.

- *Make it visual.* Very few people want to stare at a blank document with no visual aids. Use appropriate graphs to dress up your reports and show the story your data are telling you. Additionally, use templates found in word processors to showcase your information. Using call-out quotes, graphs, photos, and text help you and your audience, exhibiting your professionalism and allowing the reader to appreciate the significance of your project.

- *Make sure to use the right graphs.* Although this advice may seem trite, many times teachers will use incorrect graphing techniques when trying to tell the story of their data. Take a moment and determine if your choice in graph (histogram, line, pie, bar) is the best option to show your data. Also, ensure that it tells the accurate picture of your data and does not lead to other assumptions.

- *Get it edited.* This document sums up your entire project. Make sure it is picture perfect and something you are proud to show to others. Even if a colleague is not proficient in data, you should ask him or her to review your report before submission to ensure that it is generally understandable, readable, and approachable.

Look in the appendixes for examples of reports provided to multiple users on the completion of grant projects and to put your ideas into practice.

Sixth-Period Review Guide

✎ When including statistics in your proposal, make sure to do the following:
- Do your research.
- Include relevant information.
- Know your audience.
- Cite your data correctly.

✎ Quantitative data are measures of values or counts and are expressed as numbers.

✎ Qualitative data are measures of types and can be represented by a name, symbol, or number code.

✎ A high-quality assessment plan combines the use of qualitative and quantitative measures.

✎ The four items to keep in mind when collecting data are as follows:
- Stay on schedule.
- Stick to your plan.
- Keep it legal.
- Get permission.

✎ You should never make a change that will dramatically alter the project from what was originally proposed, even if you never have to provide follow-up data to the funder.

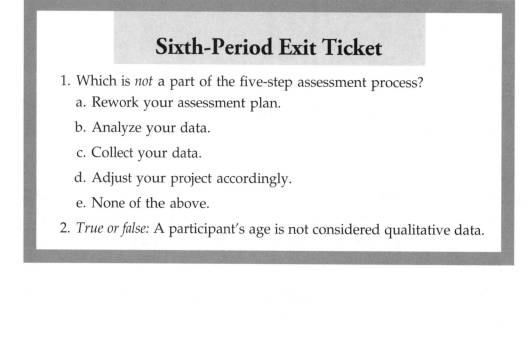

Sixth-Period Exit Ticket

1. Which is *not* a part of the five-step assessment process?
   a. Rework your assessment plan.
   b. Analyze your data.
   c. Collect your data.
   d. Adjust your project accordingly.
   e. None of the above.

2. *True or false:* A participant's age is not considered qualitative data.

Seventh Period: Communication

Your grant has officially been submitted. Now you wait . . . and wait. Finally, the day comes when you receive an e-mail from the funding organization. The subject says, "Your Grant Application Status," and you slowly move your mouse over the e-mail and click to read . . .

We hope the e-mail starts off with "Congratulations!" or "Your grant application has been funded!" Many times, though, the e-mail contains the information you were dreading, that the organization "received several quality submissions, but unfortunately" your grant proposal was not funded.

Whether your application was rejected or approved, there are a few more steps to the grant-writing process. These steps are outlined in this chapter, and we will give you a few suggestions for creative ways to thank your funder and reach out to potential granting organizations for future projects. Although this chapter may not contain information on actually writing the grant proposal, the follow-up and communication you have with your funder and all your stakeholders after you have submitted your proposal will often affect the overall experience of the project and correlate to future funding opportunities.

Thanking All Involved

Before you find out whether your proposal was funded or not, it is important to personally thank everyone who helped you along the way. If you work in the same school or office, send personalized messages, thanking that person for exactly what he or she did to assist you when you were working on the proposal; do not send a mass e-mail. If there are people who helped whom you may call on again for future proposals, make sure to show them that you really appreciate their work! Flowers, a small gift card, or breakfast before school can go a long way when you ask them for their help in the future!

> Make copies of everything and keep them for your records. Your supervisor may want a copy of your proposal, acceptance letter, and any other documents you have submitted. Additionally, over time, your skills as a grant writer will improve. Keeping old grants, awarded or not, and reviewing them at a later date is an excellent reflective exercise and will help to hone your ability over time.

Make sure to also notify your direct supervisor that the final proposal has been submitted, and send him or her a copy of the final proposal. If you are a teacher, this should be your grade-level head, department chair, and your administrative team. If you were working as part of a teacher team, make sure that each team member receives the final draft and notification of the submission. Check with your principal or administrative team, because sometimes school districts have certain regulations about who needs to be notified when a grant has been submitted (or when funding is awarded). Some school districts will require you to notify the school or district business manager and even the local school board. Keeping everyone up-to-date will increase the collaboration for the program if your proposal is ultimately funded.

If you partnered with a community organization or another outside entity, make sure to notify the organization that the final proposal has been submitted and that you will contact them of the final decision once you hear from the funder. Sometimes it is appropriate to share the final proposal with your partnering organizations, depending on the scope of the partnership.

The Dreaded Rejection Letter

Your grant proposal will end in one of two ways: a rejection letter or an award letter (followed by a check). We hope, after reading this book and putting the strategies you have learned into practice, you will start to receive more award letters than rejection letters.

Rejection letters can be disheartening. You just put in hours and hours of work into writing a needs statement, project description, budget, and evaluation, and now you are right back to where you started: a great idea for a project and no funds to implement it. Frustration, sadness, and apathy are all common emotions after hearing that your proposal was not funded. We have been there! Don't worry, because those emotions go away and soon you will be refocused and energized for your students and school.

Even the best grant writers receive their fair share of rejection letters. You can write a fantastic proposal, but so can someone else, and it comes down to the opinion of the reviewing panel. Because all foundations have a limited amount of funds allocated for grant awards, not all proposals will be funded, and receiving rejection letters is just a part of the process. It doesn't mean you are a bad grant writer or will never win a grant, so keep your head up and focus on your next proposal.

Even with a rejection letter, your work is not done. After receiving the rejection letter, you still need to follow up with a thank-you letter to the granting organization. We know it sounds a little awkward to thank someone who denied your request; you have probably never written a thank-you letter to someone who turned you down when asking him or her on a date, but with grant writing, it is best to stay professional and keep future options open. Your letter should be brief and sincere. We recommend waiting a few days after you receive the rejection letter to let your emotions return to a normal state before writing your thank-you letter. Read the following letter for an example of a post-rejection letter.

> Even the best grant writers receive their fair share of rejection letters.

EXAMPLE

Example of a Thank-You Letter after Receiving a Rejection Letter

Columbus High School
Home of the Cougars
234 Freemont Drive
Austin, Texas
555-334-2459

November 9, 2013
Attn: STARS Grant Review Committee
XYZ Organization

On behalf of the students of Room 104 at Columbus High School in Austin, Texas, I would like to thank you for the opportunity to apply for the STARS classroom grant. The students enjoyed brainstorming and creating the class project submitted in the proposal. The experience of planning, researching, and writing the proposal was highly beneficial for me as an educator. My students and I look forward to applying for future funding from your organization.

Thank you and your organization for your commitment to education.

Professionally,
Mr. Reginald Weeks
Biology teacher
Columbus High School

A quick e-mail to all stakeholders, partners, and your supervisors stating that your proposal was not funded and thanking them again is also necessary. If you have immediate plans to pursue other funding for this project, you can also mention your plans in this e-mail.

Depending on the type of grant you applied for (foundation, state, federal, etc.), you may be able to call the organization or agency and ask for some feedback about your proposal. Some foundations will be more than happy to share your final numerical score or reviewer comments with you. Other foundations that offer smaller grants and do not have a very large staff may not have the time or resources to give each application feedback. When inquiring about feedback, be polite and take the "my school is curious about how we can improve our proposal for future submissions" approach. By law (Freedom of Information Act), federal agencies must give you feedback on your proposal if you request it; however, the time it takes to receive this feedback varies on the number of submissions and staffing of the department. Use any information you receive to review your submitted application and make improvements for future submissions. The best grant writers, much like the best teachers, are reflective and continuously strive to improve their craft.

Victory: The Award Letter

One of the highlights of our careers has been reading the words "Congratulations, your grant proposal has been chosen to be funded!" With this short little sentence comes a rush of emotions and adrenaline. Knowing that all the hard work you and your team just placed into writing this grant was worth it and is a big relief and cause for celebration! After you celebrate, though, it is time to get back to work! Before you dive into your implementation plan and timeline, you need to take a moment to thank the funder and notify all stakeholders that your proposal was approved.

Although this thank-you letter should also be short and sincere, it needs to give the funder your immediate next steps as well. Take a look at the following example letter thanking an organization after a funded application.

Example of a Thank-You Letter after Receiving an Award Letter

Columbus High School
Home of the Cougars
234 Freemont Drive
Austin, Texas
555-334-2459

November 9, 2013
Attn: Mrs. Yolanda Jackson
Director of XYZ Organization

On behalf of the students of Room 104 at Columbus High School in Austin, Texas, I would like to thank you for selecting our project, "Students 4 College," to be funded. Your financial commitment will ensure the project's implementation and overall success. The students and I are eager and excited to get started on the initial steps of the project, which include selecting two state universities and two out-of-state universities to research and visit. My students and I are looking forward to updating you on the progress and results of "Students 4 College."

Thank you and your organization for your commitment to education.

Professionally,
Mr. Reginald Weeks
Biology teacher
Columbus High School

Remember all those people you thanked right after you submitted your proposal? Now it is time to go back and tell them the good news! Depending on the number of people who helped you construct your proposal, an e-mail, phone call, or memo is appropriate. People like being part of a successful project, so let them know that their work was not in vain, and they will be more likely to help you again in the future.

Next, you will need to contact all partners and stakeholders from the proposal. If you decided to partner with the botanical garden, as mentioned in chapter 3, make sure you reach out to your contact person and let him or her know that the project is a go! You don't have to start setting dates for meetings, speakers, or working out the details of a field trip just yet; simply notify your partners that your program was funded and that you will be in touch in the near future to start working on implementation. Sometimes, when a communication about a winning application is mixed with immediate business steps, it can take away from that emotional high of being a part of a successful team. Let each stakeholder have that moment of relief, excitement, and success, and then in a few days or a week, reach out again to get the ball rolling.

Ongoing Communication and Updates

Either the award letter or the follow-up letter from the granting organization will remind you of the specific deadlines to submit updates and your final evaluation. Write these dates everywhere—in your calendar, in an e-mail to yourself, on a sticky note stuck in your sock drawer—whatever you need to do so that you do not miss these deadlines!

In your proposal, you should have described your assessment and evaluation plan in detail. In this section we hope you also identified the data and results that you would be sharing with the granting organization. Some funders will have specific forms or surveys for you to complete. Others will just want regular updates on the progress, budget, and anticipated time left to complete your objectives. The key is to follow the guidelines of the granting organization. Many times for education-related grants under $5,000, a simple report detailing the achievement of the objectives will suffice.

Depending on the size and type of your project, we have identified some common items that you can send to the funding organization at the conclusion of your project or program:

Single Classroom Project or Unit

- Student data report showing increase or growth in relation to your proposal's objectives
- Sample of completed student work (essay, creation of book, blueprint of dream house, college acceptance letters)
- Copies of all assessments with a report detailing results of each assessment
- All receipts and final budget report

Extended Classroom Project or Unit with Outside School Partner

- Proof of partnership with outside partner (itinerary of field trip, handouts from organization)

- Report detailing how partnership with outside organization added value to unit or program in correlation to proposal's objectives

Schoolwide Program or After-school Program

- Number of applications for program versus number selected to prove rigorous entry or selectivity
- Report identifying growth of students enrolled in program versus similar students who were not enrolled in the program

School District Initiative or Districtwide Program

- Evidence of systemwide impact such as aggregate growth among participants
- A comprehensive booklet-style report detailing not only the overall outcomes and activities of the project but also individual school-based snapshots

Multiyear Programming with One or More Outside School Partners

- Timelines showing yearly progress toward the goals and objectives with projections on future outcomes
- Digital media that allow a reader to explore the many partners and their role in your shared work

> If you are ever unsure of what the granting organization needs from you, call the program officer and clarify. Now that your proposal has been funded, it is important for you to maintain communication with the organization and submit all forms and data necessary. If you are in the middle of a multiple-phase or multiyear grant, failure to adhere to deadlines could result in a cancellation of remaining funds.

In addition to sending the updates and final evaluation report to the granting organization, be sure to share final data and results with all stakeholders involved. Let people in your school community know what you and your students did! A successfully funded and completed program can be a great component for your principal to add to his or her end-of-year report (not to mention score you some extra bonus points!)! If your school or school district has an e-mail listserv that sends updates to the school community and

Make sure to mention the granting organization in any form of media you release about the project and then send them a copy!

stakeholders, submit an article about your funded project and include the results and a picture of your students. Don't be shy; let everyone know how hard you and your students worked to receive free money and then used it to create something awesome for your students and school!

Here is a list of great ideas for follow-up communication to the funder, stakeholders, and school community:

- Have students write an article for the school paper or local newspaper about the project.

- Contact a local radio station to do a quick, two-minute story about your students and their project.

- Have each student write a personal thank-you letter to the granting organization and all partners.

- Take a picture of all participants at the end of the project, and send it to the funder and stakeholders. Having the students hold something they completed would be even better!

- Send your partners or funder an "honorary member of room 309" certificate signed by all the students.

- Make a picture timeline of the entire project and have students make comments under each picture to hang up in your school or partner organization's office.

- Reach out to a local politician for a visit on the final day of the program (any politician will see this as an excellent photo shoot with students and community interaction), and then send a picture of the politician and your students to the funder for some major bonus points.

Whichever way you choose to follow up with your funders and stakeholders, do not undervalue the use of narrative. People enjoy the journey just as much as the end result. Try to work in personal and organizational narratives into all reporting through photos, quotes from participants, and other media that will connect a reader to your project. Use technology and build a website, wiki, Prezi presentation, or any other kind of format that would allow you to embed video and sound into a report that is able to be sent out. Upload videos and slideshows that showcase your work. Using the tradition of storytelling goes a long way when forging a stronger relationship with a funder.

Building a Relationship with Your Funder and Other Stakeholders

It has been stressed throughout this book that building a relationship among you, your school, and a funder is a key component to the success of your proposal. Funders are people, too, and they are certainly interested in more than the financial transaction that just took place. Oftentimes, we find that a teacher has a closer relationship with the barista at the local coffee shop than the program officer who just provided the teacher with $10,000!

Similar to any relationship, it takes work, dedication, persistence, and perseverance to build a long-lasting "marriage" between you and your stakeholders. Here are a few tips that will help you build a strong connection with others and may result in future funding:

- *Don't neglect your stakeholders.* Even if your funder only requires periodic or structured reporting, be sure to include the funder on newsletters, event invites, and other means of connecting. Funders may never respond to you or may never be able to make it to an event, but they will most certainly be reading your communications and feel a stronger connection to your school.

- *Provide a space for them to get involved.* Get creative and include all stakeholders (especially funders) in your project in an authentic way. Perhaps you purchased books to build a reading café . . . could you invite your funder or parents to read to students one evening? Maybe the grant funds a debate team . . . is there a way you can include them in your practices? The more active stakeholders are in your project, the more likely they will develop a deep relationship with your school.

- *Discuss other projects.* This can be delicate, because you do not want to badger funders with new ideas every time you talk with them. Instead, try and talk about other projects that they are working on or that you have recently heard about in the area. A conversation that starts with "Did you hear what they are doing out east?" might very well turn into "Well, we should do that here!"

- *Be friendly.* At the end of the day, people want to enjoy their jobs. By being friendly and approachable, your stakeholders will want to be around you more, giving you more opportunities to network. Take a genuine interest in them and try to sprinkle in conversation that is not just about work when appropriate.

Relationship building can lead to additional funding for future projects or, more important, continued funding for your same project. Because many grants are one-time payments, it is difficult to continue year after year when money has dried up. Building relationships with various stakeholders creates a stronger likelihood that someone will want to make a long-term investment and sustain your project.

Thinking about the Future

If you are like us, as soon as you submit your first proposal, you will begin to start thinking about writing your next grant. Now that you know where to find grants, how to navigate an RFP, how to choose your writing style, and how to construct each section of the proposal, you will be constantly searching for grants to fund more projects for your classroom, school, or district.

If you have a grant that has funded only part of your project or will provide only enough funding for the first year of a multiyear project, you should continue looking for funding to sustain your project. You can certainly have conversations with your current funder about continuing but it is good practice to have back-up plans that may include approaching other potential funders and applying for new RFPs. One common technique is to make a small tweak to a program or project before applying to a new funder. See the following example.

> You have been awarded funds to support an after-school robotics team. The funds cover only the first year but you intend to keep the robotics team going in the future. Your administration has promised to provide money for supplies once grant dollars run out next year but you still need funds for travel, a teacher stipend, extra help, and other program costs. Your current funder has indicated that the organization hands out only one-year grants and will not continue to fund you after this year.
>
> You find a new RFP that looks to increase science scores in middle school–aged children and want to apply but your program only works with high school students. You decide to apply to the grant and expand your program by offering a seventh- and eighth-grade extension program in which once a month, your high school students go to the local middle school and work with their students on early robotics training.
>
> You are able to report your year-one findings on the new RFP as further justification as to why the program should grow to the middle school and useful statistics about increasing science scores, meanwhile creating an effective transition between eighth grade and freshman year.

We encourage you to avoid basing new projects off of RFPs you come across in your search. Instead, search for RFPs that align to the units or programming you currently have with your students and the needs in your school and district. If you find an RFP that will fund an after-school science program, and you see a need for growth in science scores, by all means go for it! We just recommend you don't write an RFP for a specific program that doesn't align to the needs of your classroom or school. Think about what would happen if you wrote a proposal to receive funding for a Saturday school trilingual program in which students would have the opportunity to learn French and German. It sounds like a fantastic opportunity for students, but if your school needs help with literacy in English, putting staff hours and commitment into a program that doesn't align to your needs, just because you won a grant, may be more of a hindrance than an opportunity.

We know that you are busy lesson planning, grading papers, analyzing student data, communicating with parents, and finding some time to sleep. As teachers, we try to have a set time every other week or once month that we spend researching available RFPs. Bookmark links to organizations

> Search for RFPs that align to the units or programming you currently have.

or online RFPs that you think you may want to apply for in the future. Create a list categorized by month of when revolving grants become available and their deadlines. Try to write one proposal per academic year to stay up-to-date on current RFPs and hone your grant-writing skills. A few teachers in our organization dedicate their entire summer to writing proposals for the coming school year!

Writing grants can be stressful, time consuming, and mentally draining but when you realize that you have the power to receive free money for your students, the grant-writing process becomes addicting. Check out appendix B for full examples of submitted grant proposals, and refer back to the chapters in this book as often as you need. We look forward to reading your future proposal for the UNITE Classroom Grant! Happy writing!

Seventh-Period Review Guide

🖉 Before you even hear back from the granting organization about the status of your proposal, thank everyone who helped you during the process. Your appreciation of their help goes a long way!

🖉 Rejection letters happen to all grant writers. You will live through it! Still take a moment to professionally thank the granting organization for the opportunity to apply for the grant.

🖉 Enjoy the feeling of success after the award letter! Notify everyone involved that the proposal was funded! Professionally thank the funding organization for the opportunity and award.

🖉 Make sure to meet all deadlines of communication with your funder.

🖉 Think of some creative ways to thank the granting organization and publicize your program.

🖉 Don't stop! Keep searching for RFPs, writing proposals, and winning grants!

Seventh-Period Exit Ticket

1. *True or false:* A thank-you letter to the funding organization is necessary even if you were not awarded the grant.

2. List two ways you can recognize and thank a funder in addition to your initial thank-you letter.

Appendix A: Templates and Worksheets

To download many of the templates and worksheets from this book, go to
www.wiley.com/go/educationgrants

Project or Program Planning Template

This planning template can be used during the initial stages of the grant-writing process to formulate your ideas. If you are working with a team, have each member complete this template individually and then bring to the first meeting to guide your discussion.

Identify a Problem or Need Conduct research about the problems you see in your classroom, school, district, or community. *Example:* Forty percent of ninth-grade students are not on track to graduate within the Dale County School District.	What is your problem or need?
Goal Goals are long-term, overarching targets that can be reached by continuous dedication and perseverance. Most classroom grants under $5,000 will not ask you for an overarching goal; rather, specific objectives. *Example:* The Dale County School District will have 85 percent of all ninth-grade students on track to graduate within two academic years as measured by state requirements.	What is your goal?

Objectives

Objectives are outcomes that can be measured within a given time frame. A series of objectives help you keep focused and strive for the overall goal.

Refer back to chapter 3 for the five essentials for writing objectives:

- Alignment
- Participants
- Time
- Results
- Measurable

Example: Ninety percent of ninth-grade students will pass all their academic courses during the first semester.

What are your objectives?

Project or program

The project or program is the step-by-step plan that you and your students or the school district is going to take in order to meet each objective and your overall goal. What specific lessons or programs will you implement to meet your objectives? What strategies and resources will be used in order to attain your desired outcomes?

Example: Students who are identified as at-risk for not being on track to graduate on entering ninth grade will participate in a weekly mentoring session with a ninth-grade teacher. These mentoring sessions will be used to monitor student behavior, work on homework or projects, and provide incentives for attendance and grades.

What are some components of your project or program?

Proficient Example: Needs Statement

Read the following needs statement, written in 2008 by undergraduate students on the campus of Illinois State University in conjunction with UNITE and the Chicago Teacher Education Pipeline. Then complete the needs statement checklist using evidence from the example, which is a section of a larger grant.

The root problem our proposal will address is the widening of the achievement gap and low representation of low-income minority students in higher education. To effectively serve the state of Illinois in the future, higher education as a whole must adapt to the increasing diversity of the state's college-bound population. By 2014, historically underrepresented groups will comprise approximately 40% of the high school graduating class, compared to 29% in 2001–02. The Black, non-Hispanic, college-age population will remain largely stable while the number of Hispanic graduates will double. Moreover, the National Center for Educational Statistics reports substantial gaps in educational attainment across income and ethnic groups (Horn & Berger, 2004). These gaps demonstrate the need for institutions to address both access to and retention in higher education for underrepresented groups.

Research has identified common obstacles to academic achievement for first-generation college students. These obstacles include lack of self-confidence (Terenzini et al., 1996), inappropriate expectations about college (Werner-Smith & Smolin, 1995), lack of connection to the college community and validation from it (Garcia, 2001), limited cultural context (Garcia, 2001), and limited support from family members who also do not understand college requirements and expectations (Brazziel & Brazziel, 1995). According to Mow and Nettles (1990), attitudinal factors and college experiences relate to student success, particularly for African American students.

Needs Statement Checklist

☐ *Clear explanation of the problem or challenge facing the proposer*

Evidence from text:

_____

_____

_____

_____

☐ *Insight into the classroom, school, and community with current student and school data*

Evidence from text:

_____

_____

_____

_____

☐ *Anecdotal evidence that allows the reader to connect to the proposer's students and school*

Evidence from text:

_____

_____

_____

_____

☐ *Data and research to support the problem, challenge, and anecdotal evidence*

Evidence from text:

_____

_____

_____

_____

☐ *Connection to a larger-scale problem or consequence*

Evidence from text:

_____

_____

_____

_____

Example of a Likert Survey Template

Title of survey: _____

Directions to participant: Please respond to each of the following statements by circling one number from the columns on the right. Your responses will be anonymous and the results of your individual survey will not be included in the final report. All participant responses will be averaged together to assess the desired outcome.

Statements	Strongly agree	Agree	Neutral	Disagree	Strongly disagree
1.	5	4	3	2	1
2.	5	4	3	2	1
3.	5	4	3	2	1
4.	5	4	3	2	1
5.	5	4	3	2	1
6.	5	4	3	2	1
7.	5	4	3	2	1
8.	5	4	3	2	1
9.	5	4	3	2	1
10.	5	4	3	2	1
11.	5	4	3	2	1
12.	5	4	3	2	1
13.	5	4	3	2	1
14.	5	4	3	2	1
15.	5	4	3	2	1
16.	5	4	3	2	1
17.	5	4	3	2	1
18.	5	4	3	2	1
19.	5	4	3	2	1
20.	5	4	3	2	1

Thank you for your participation in this survey.

Practice Worksheet: Word Count I

Use the selected section of the following grant proposal to practice working on word-count requirements. The given proposal section has a total of 237 words, but the prompt states that the response should have a maximum of 200 words. Use the next page to rewrite the section using a maximum of 200 words. Make sure to still answer all components of the question prompt. Feel free to cross out words, use editing symbols, and make notes as you read and decide how to rewrite the proposal. These sections are adapted from a funded proposal written by elementary bilingual teacher and UNITE member Carmela Balice. You can find an example on page 153 of how this section was condensed to 200 words to compare with your revisions!

Prompt: Describe your classroom and your students. Identify a problem or need that your students face during the school day. Responses should not exceed 200 words.

My classroom consists of 26 third graders, 13 boys and 13 girls, all of whom are Hispanic. One student receives additional services in speech while another has a 504 Plan for an asthma related health condition. All of the students in my class are part of the free breakfast and lunch program. Due to the fact that my students are low-income, many of them eat the meals provided by the school which are not always the most nutritious. My students are only provided with physical education one time a week for forty minutes. In addition to this time, students are only allowed two days a week to have recess if classroom time permits. While at recess, students have no equipment to play with and spend most of the time sitting down due to boredom. The result of these factors is that my students are taking in unhealthy amounts of fat and sugar while having few options to exercise and ensure their healthiness. If granted the money to complete this project, students will be given more opportunities to be active during recess. Equipment will be provided to students in order for them to participate in both educational and team building related games which will encourage them to be more active. If students are encouraged to be more active and have fun in the process, they will develop healthy lifestyle habits and will continue these habits long into their future.

Rewrite the response making sure to stay within the 200-word limit while still answering all components of the original prompt.

_____
_____
_____
_____
_____
_____
_____
_____
_____
_____
_____
_____
_____
_____
_____
_____
_____
_____
_____
_____
_____
_____
_____
_____
_____
_____
_____
_____
_____
_____
_____
_____
_____
_____

Practice Worksheet: Word Count II

Use the selected section of the following grant proposal to practice working on word-count requirements. The given proposal section has a total of 223 words, but the prompt states that the response should have a maximum of 200 words. Use the next page to rewrite the section using a maximum of 200 words. Make sure to still answer all components of the question prompt. Feel free to cross out words, use editing symbols, and make notes as you read and decide how to rewrite the proposal. You can find an example on page 154 of how this section was condensed to 200 words compare with your revisions!

Prompt: How will your project be measured using data? Please describe how you will determine the success of your project or program. Responses should not exceed 200 words.

Project PLAY incorporates student learning outcomes that are measurable and can be supported with data. The learning outcomes will be measured by surveying students, teachers, and parents. In order to provide aggregate data from Project PLAY, a survey will be taken by students and teachers prior to the project and after the completion of the playground. Participants will rate statements concerning the impact of the playground space on students. These statements will be answered using a 1–10 Likert scale where participants will agree or disagree with each statement. Participants will be surveyed on topics concerning active engagement, conflict resolution skills, academic skill development, and safety of activities during recess. These surveys will be used to gather data in order to determine the impact Project PLAY had on students. The teachers' responses will be measured as one subgroup and the students as another. Once Project PLAY has been completed, teachers and students will be asked to complete an identical survey. These responses will then be gathered and the data will be placed into a bar identical to the first. After comparing the responses, the data will indicate that the improvement in the recess area had a positive impact on both students and teachers. Using this data will demonstrate the positive impact Project PLAY had on both the students and teachers throughout the school.

Rewrite the response making sure to stay within the 200-word limit while still answering all components of the original prompt.

_____
_____
_____
_____
_____
_____
_____
_____
_____
_____
_____
_____
_____
_____
_____
_____
_____
_____
_____
_____
_____
_____
_____
_____
_____
_____
_____
_____
_____
_____
_____
_____
_____
_____
_____

Practice Worksheet: Needs Statement

Use the following school and classroom facts to create a needs statement in response to the given prompt. Refer back to the needs statement checklist from chapter 3, which is restated in the following. Make sure that your needs statement has all five components from the checklist. Feel free to provide other information, such as anecdotal evidence or specific percentages, not given in the following when writing your needs statement. You can find an example needs statement based on these same school and classroom facts on page 155. Compare your needs statement to this example when you are finished!

School and classroom facts	Needs statement checklist
• High-needs, urban school in New York, NY • Special education teacher • Three different periods of the day • Twenty-nine total students • Students in grades 6, 7, and 8 • All students are below reading level; most are three to four grade levels behind. • Students are disengaged due to a lack of age-appropriate and interesting reading texts for middle school students that they can read with accuracy and fluency.	☐ Clear explanation of the problem or challenge ☐ Insight into the classroom, school, and community with current student and school data ☐ Anecdotal evidence that allows the reader to connect to the proposer's students and school ☐ Data and research to support the problem ☐ Connection to a larger-scale problem or consequence

Prompt: Describe your classroom. What needs do your students have? How will your project address those needs?

_____

_____

_____

_____

_____

_____

_____

_____

_____

_____

Practice Worksheet: Budget Categories: Fourth Period

The following items represent line items that need to be included in a budget proposal. Correctly place each line item in the appropriate section of the budget shown on page 150. Compare your results to the example provided on page 157.

Items

- 16 boxes of copy paper—$13.00/box
- Bus rental – Acme Charters—$1,000*
- Mentor teacher stipend—$2,300
- Postage and envelopes—$150
- 4 steel work tables—$250 per table

- 1 high-output copy machine—$3,000
- Assorted hand tools—$700
- Assorted lumber—$550
- Catering for exhibition—$400
- Indirect costs to school—7.0 percent of total

* Similar to a real scenario, some assumptions must be made when filling in missing information. For example, the bus rental is an estimate as well as catering. In this example, the applicant simply listed a conservative estimate of how much those items will actually cost and budgeted accordingly.

Quantity	Description	Summary	Unit cost	Total cost
			Subtotal	$
			Indirect @ 7.00%	$
			Tax (exempt)	0.00%
			Total	**$**

Practice Worksheet: Ledger Activity: Fifth Period

Correctly place the following items into the ledger on page 152. Follow the example provided in chapter 5. Compare your results to the example provided on page 160.

Transactions

- On Oct. 1, you receive your first of two checks from your funder for $17,000.
- You order volleyball uniforms for $4,597 from LaDon's Closet on Oct. 6.
- On Oct. 7, you purchase forty volleyballs from Sports Inc. for $417.
- You receive the uniforms previously purchased on Oct. 28.
- You pay a deposit of $600 for a gym rental at the YMCA on Nov. 3 for an upcoming conference.
- You purchase $1,000 worth of concessions goods to be sold at the conference on Nov. 3.
- On Nov. 4, you pay for the buses for your school in the amount of $700.
- A parent donates $40 to the team as you get on the bus on Nov. 6.
- At the conference (Nov. 6), you pay the remaining YMCA rental of $5,400.
- At the end of the night, you pay staff who took tickets, work concessions, provided security, operated parking, and guided teams around to total $5,000 (Nov. 6).
- You pay referees on Nov. 6 a total of $1,500 for their services.
- On Nov. 7, you pay $150 to the YMCA for a broken window your volleyball player made while practicing spikes against a wall.
- On Nov. 7, you deposit $1,500 from concession sales.
- On Nov. 7, you deposit $500 from ticket sales.
- On Nov. 15, you receive your second and final check from the funder for $3,000.
- On Nov. 16, you throw a party for volleyball players and boosters to celebrate first place and spend $676 on food and decorations.
- On Nov. 30, a check written by your administrator is paid to you for your hard work in the amount of $2,000 using funds from this account. (Was it worth it?)

Date	Description	Credit	Debit	Balance

Answer Worksheet: Word Counts I and II

Use the two passages below that have been trimmed down to meet the 200-word limit requirement. Compare these two sections to the practice word-count worksheets. Pay close attention to what was deleted or reworded in the following sections so that the question prompt was still fully answered. These sections are adapted from a funded proposal written by elementary bilingual teacher and UNITE member Carmela Balice.

Answer Worksheet: Word Count I

Prompt: Describe your classroom and your students. Identify a problem or need that your students face during the school day. Responses should not exceed 200 words.

My classroom consists of 26 third graders, ~~13 boys and 13 girls~~, all of whom are Hispanic. ~~One student receives additional services in speech while another has a 504 Plan for an asthma related health condition~~. All of the students in my class are part of the free breakfast and lunch program. Due to the fact that my students are low-income, many of them eat the meals provided by the school which are not always the most nutritious. My students are only provided with physical education one time a week for forty minutes. In addition to this time, students are only allowed two days a week to have recess if classroom time permits. While at recess, students have no equipment to play with and spend most of the time sitting down due to boredom. The result ~~of these factors~~ is that my students are taking in unhealthy amounts of fat and sugar while having few options to exercise and ensure their healthiness. If ~~granted the money to complete this~~ **MY** project **IS FUNDED**, students will be given ~~more~~ opportunities to be active during recess. Equipment will be provided to students in order for them to participate in both educational and team building related games ~~which will encourage them to be more active~~. If students are encouraged to be more active and have fun in the process, they will develop healthy lifestyle habits and will continue these habits long into their future.

Final Word Count: 199

Answer Worksheet: Word Count II

Prompt: How will your project be measured using data? Please describe how you will determine the success of your project or program. Responses should not exceed 200 words.

Project PLAY incorporates student learning outcomes that are measurable and can be supported with data. The learning outcomes will be measured by surveying students, teachers, and parents. In order to provide aggregate data from Project PLAY, a survey will be taken by students and teachers prior to the project and after the completion of the playground. Participants will rate statements concerning the impact of the playground space ~~on students. These statements will be answered~~ using a 1–10 Likert scale where participants will agree or disagree with each statement. Participants will be surveyed on topics concerning active engagement, conflict resolution skills, academic skill development, and safety of activities during recess. These surveys will be used to gather data in order to determine the impact Project PLAY had on students. The teachers' responses will be measured as one subgroup and the students as another. Once Project PLAY has been completed, teachers and students will be asked to complete an identical survey. ~~These responses will then be gathered and the data will be placed into a bar identical to the first.~~ After comparing the responses, the data will indicate that the improvement in the recess area had a positive impact on both students and teachers. Using this data will demonstrate the positive impact Project PLAY had on both the students and teachers throughout the school.

Final Word Count: 197

Answer Worksheet: Needs Statement

Use the following needs statement to compare with your needs statement from the practice worksheet. This needs statement was adapted from a grant proposal written by Rachel Perveiler, a special education teacher and UNITE member. Her project was fully funded by UNITE in 2011. Does Rachel's need statement meet all the requirements based on the following checklist? Does your needs statement reflect some components of Rachel's needs statement?

School and classroom facts	Needs statement checklist
• High-needs, urban school in New York, NY	☐ Clear explanation of the problem or challenge
• Special education teacher	☐ Insight into the classroom, school, and community with current student and school data
• Three different periods of the day	
• Twenty-nine total students	☐ Anecdotal evidence that allows the reader to connect to the proposer's students and school
• Students in grades 6, 7, and 8	
• All students are below reading level; most are three to four grade levels behind.	☐ Data and research to support the problem
• Students are disengaged due to a lack of age-appropriate and interesting reading texts for middle school students that they can read with accuracy and fluency.	☐ Connection to a larger-scale problem or consequence

Prompt: Describe your classroom. What needs do your students have? How will your project address those needs?

At Shepard Academy 55%, 64%, and 57% of sixth, seventh, and eighth graders respectively are reading below grade level. Shepard's network of nearby elementary schools averages 65% of students below grade level. Many students in New York require intense intervention to make reading gains. Students lacking reading ability inhibit growth during high stakes testing and even generations later, when students' families lack reading ability. According to Reading Rockets, "it is vital that children read a large amount of text at their independent reading level (with 95 percent accuracy)," to increase fluency, vocabulary, and comprehension. At Shepard, most public libraries, or homes, students struggle to locate age-appropriate texts with which they experience 95% accuracy.

As a special educator at Shepard Academy, I service 29 middle grade (6th, 7th, and 8th) students with Individualized Education Plans (IEPs), primarily with reading learning disabilities. Several of the students read successfully at Fountas and Pinnel levels H through L, which is comparable to the reading ability of a student in second or third grade. This is the cause for many struggles such as distractibility of self and peers, bullying, low motivation, lack of homework completion, and low grades. A clear solution to this problem is expanding Shepard's selection of high-interest, beginning-level reading books. Offering high-interest books at beginning reading levels is crucial for reading progress at Shepard.

Answer Worksheet: Budget Categories: Fourth Period

The following listed items represent line items that need to be included in a budget proposal. Correctly place each line item in the appropriate section of the following budget.

Items

- 16 boxes of copy paper—$13.00/box
- Bus rental – Acme Charters—$1,000*
- Mentor teacher stipend—$2,300
- Postage and envelopes—$150
- 4 steel work tables—$250 per table

- 1 high-output copy machine—$3,000
- Assorted hand tools—$700
- Assorted lumber—$550
- Catering for exhibition—$400
- Indirect costs to school—7.0 percent of total

Quantity	Description	Summary	Unit Cost	Total Cost
16	Box of copy paper	Used for printing	$13	$208
1	Assorted lumber	For building sets	$550	$550
1	Postage and envelopes	Mailings	$150	$150
			Supply total	**$908**
1	Bus rental	Travel to regionals	$1,000	$1,000
1	Catering for exhibition	Food for main event	$400	$400
			Contractual total	**$1,400**
4	Steel work tables	Used in set shop	$250	$1,000
1	Assorted hand tools	Hammers, screwdrivers, etc.	$700	$700

1	High-output copy machine	Program printing, invites, general use	$3,000	$3,000
			Equipment total	**$4,700**
1	Mentor teacher stipend	Set building coach	$2,300	$2,300
			Personnel total	**$2,300**
			Subtotal	$9,308
			Indirect @ 7.00%	$651.56
			Tax (Exempt)	0.00%
			Total	**$9,959.56**

* Similar to a real scenario, some assumptions must be made when filling in missing information. For example, the bus rental is an estimate as well as catering. In this example, the applicant simply listed a conservative estimate of how much those items will actually cost and budgeted accordingly.

Answer Worksheet: Ledger Activity: Fifth Period

Correctly place the items below into the ledger. Follow the example provided in chapter 5.

Transactions

- On Oct. 1, you receive your first of two checks from your funder for $17,000.
- You order volleyball uniforms for $4,597 from LaDon's Closet on Oct. 6.
- On Oct. 7, you purchase forty volleyballs from Sports Inc. for $417.
- You receive the uniforms previously purchased on Oct. 28.
- You pay a deposit of $600 for a gym rental at the YMCA on Nov. 3 for an upcoming conference.
- You purchase $1,000 worth of concessions goods to be sold at the conference on Nov. 3.
- On Nov. 4, you pay for the buses for your school in the amount of $700.
- A parent donates $40 to the team as you get on the bus on Nov. 6.
- At the conference (Nov. 6), you pay the remaining YMCA rental of $5,400.
- At the end of the night, you pay staff who took tickets, work concessions, provided security, operated parking, and guided teams around to total $5,000 (Nov. 6).
- You pay referees on Nov. 6 a total of $1,500 for their services.
- On Nov. 7, you pay $150 to the YMCA for a broken window your volleyball player made while practicing spikes against a wall.
- On Nov. 7, you deposit $1,500 from concession sales.
- On Nov. 7, you deposit $500 from ticket sales.
- On Nov. 15, you receive your second and final check from the funder for $3,000.
- On Nov. 16, you throw a party for volleyball players and boosters to celebrate first place and spend $676 on food and decorations.
- On Nov. 30, a check written by your administrator is paid to you for your hard work in the amount of $2,000 using funds from this account. (Was it worth it?)

Date	Description	Credit	Debit	Balance
10/1/15	First installment – UNITE, NFP	$17,000		$17,000
10/6/15	Uniforms – LaDon's Closet		$4,597	$12,403
10/7/15	Volleyballs – Sports Inc.		$417	$11,986
11/3/15	Deposit for space – YMCA		$600	$11,386
11/3/15	Concession goods		$1,000	$10,386
11/4/15	Bus rental – School district		$700	$9,686
11/6/15	Parent cash donation	$40		$9,726
11/6/15	Space rental – YMCA		$5,400	$4,326
	Staff payments		$5,000	($674)
	Referee payments		$1,500	($2,174)
11/7/15	Broken window repair – YMCA		$150	($2,324)
11/7/15	Concession sales revenue	$1500		($824)
11/7/15	Ticket sales revenue	$500		($324)
11/15/15	Second installment, UNITE, NFP	$3,000		$2,676
11/16/15	Celebration food and decoration		$636	$2,040
11/30/15	Coach's stipend		$2,000	$40

Appendix B: Resources

Comprehensive Chapter Review Guide

This is a comprehensive list of each chapter's review guide. This is a great resource to refresh what you read from this book and to review certain chapters in pursuit of your next grant-writing experience!

First-Period Review Guide

- Grants are monetary awards used to establish, implement, or sustain a project or program.
- Three categories of grants are rolling deadlines, revolving deadlines, and one-time awards.
- Grants are right around the corner! Foundations, corporations, nonprofit organizations, businesses, and the government all offer education grants.
- When searching online, use specific search criteria and focus on your geographic area. Don't forget to use social media to your advantage.
- Review the key terminology found in RFPs and grant applications.
- Each RFP is unique, but most contain similar terms and content.
- Most RFPs will contain the grant application questions or direct you to an electronic submission form.

Second-Period Review Guide

- Be fully prepared before you sit down to write your grant. Gather data and resources pertaining to your school or district and specific information about your proposed program.
- Follow the ten writing tips while creating your proposal:
  - Think of your proposal as a conversation with another teacher.

- Consider whether you want to use the first or third person.
- Your proposal is alive and active!
- Leave the slang on the streets.
- Your project is not "out of this world!"
- Offend no one.
- Use your English teachers.
- Make sure your points are evidence based over adjective based.
- Data always trump common knowledge.
- Be consistent.

/ All ten writing tips must be used together to create your writing style.

/ Keep track of your word and character counts.

/ Assemble your editing team early.

/ Four main components of most RFPs:
  - Needs statement or statement of need
  - Project or program description
  - Budget
  - Assessment and evaluation

Third-Period Review Guide

/ Your needs statement is an explanation of the problem or challenge facing your students, school, or district.

/ Use data to support the claims in your needs statement.

/ Connect your specific problem to a larger-scale consequence.

/ Goals are long term; objectives are the short steps taken to reach the ultimate goal.

/ Your project description is the climax of your proposal.

/ Make sure your project description answers the who, what, where, when, why, and how questions.

/ Have a focused chronological implementation plan.

/ Expand the impact of your program and make it stand out by partnering with a community organization and having a memorable name.

Fourth-Period Review Guide

/ A budget is a plan for the coordination of resources and expenditures.

/ Five best practices when shopping for goods or services are as follows:

- Go to real vendors that you know and trust.
- Shop around.
- Account for all the extras.
- Avoid private sales.
- Make best estimates when appropriate.

∕ Read grant prompts carefully and adhere to their requirements.

∕ A simple budget presentation should show the following:

- Quantity
- Description
- Product number
- Unit cost
- Total cost

∕ Never overspend your budget!

Fifth-Period Review Guide

∕ While writing the grant proposal, determine who or what entity will be the fiscal agent, that is, who will control the money.

∕ Keep an accurate log or ledger of all incoming and outgoing funds.

∕ Ensure that a trusted, independent person is also keeping a logbook to avoid errors, abuse, and questions regarding fraud.

∕ The five types of security are as follows:

- Establishment of responsibility
- Segregation of duties
- Documentation procedures
- Physical controls
- Independent internal verification

∕ Make a habit of reporting financial information to the public on a regular basis.

Sixth-Period Review Guide

∕ When including statistics in your proposal, make sure to do the following:

- Do your research.
- Include relevant information.

- Know your audience.
- Cite your data correctly.

∥ Quantitative data are measures of values or counts and are expressed as numbers.

∥ Qualitative data are measures of types and can be represented by a name, symbol, or number code.

∥ A high-quality assessment plan combines the use of qualitative and quantitative measures.

∥ The four items to keep in mind when collecting data are as follows:
- Stay on schedule.
- Stick to your plan.
- Keep it legal.
- Get permission.

∥ You should never make a change that will dramatically alter the project from what was originally proposed, even if you never have to provide follow-up data to the funder.

Seventh-Period Review Guide

∥ Before you even hear back from the granting organization about the status of your proposal, thank everyone who helped you during the process. Your appreciation of their help goes a long way!

∥ Rejection letters happen to all grant writers. You will live through it! Still take a moment to professionally thank the granting organization for the opportunity to apply for the grant.

∥ Enjoy the feeling of success after the award letter! Notify everyone involved that the proposal was funded! Professionally thank the funding organization for the opportunity and award.

∥ Make sure to meet all deadlines of communication with your funder.

∥ Think of some creative ways to thank the granting organization and publicize your program.

∥ Don't stop! Keep searching for RFPs, writing proposals, and winning grants!

Exit Ticket Answers

Use this list to check your answers to each chapter's exit ticket. The exit tickets and answers could be a great way to keep your grant-writing skills sharp or to review before you write your next proposal!

First-Period Exit Ticket Answers

1. c. Annual is not a category of a grant deadline, although most revolving grants become available on an annual basis.

2. *False*. Most RFPs will not contain information on how the granting organization will assess your proposal.

3. *False*. A business does not have to be a 501(c)3 organization to give a monetary award to a charitable organization or other entity.

Second-Period Exit Ticket Answers

1. *False*. Classroom grants under $5,000 are a great opportunity to use the first person to your advantage. Review the chart in tip 2 of chapter 2 about when to use the first versus third person.

2. *True*. Give your team plenty of time to plan ahead and time to review your proposal as you write each section.

Third-Period Exit Ticket Answers

1. d. All of these given answers must be present in a proficient needs statement, as well as anecdotal evidence and a connection to a larger-scale problem.

2. *False*. Some grant applications will not ask for either goals or objectives, but you should try to include them if possible. Not all classroom grants need to have an overall goal, but each proposal should contain specific objectives.

3. An implementation plan is a step-by-step timeline of each activity in the project in chronological order.

Fourth-Period Exit Ticket Answers

1. School personnel, granting organizations, and you are the key stakeholders. Each stakeholder has significant interest in how money is being spent. The second reason other stakeholders matter is that by viewing your budget through their lens, you have an opportunity to build a long-lasting relationship that could bring more success in the future.

2. d. Because you have paid for the work with grant funds, it cannot be considered an in-kind match. If someone else paid for the work, you could count it as a donation from that person.

Fifth-Period Exit Ticket Answers

1. The dedicated account approach is when your school creates a separate account to hold only the money related to your project. No other funds would go in and only approved project-related costs would go out. This allows for extreme control and transparency.

2. a. Physical controls. There are no physical controls securing the goods purchased.
   b. Some ideas to add physical controls would be to add identification tags to all furniture and games purchased, have a sign-in sheet for students to be completed when entering or leaving the room, create a short checklist for staff to go through before they leave the room each period that includes checking that all goods are still in the room, and ornately distinguish each product, making it more recognizable.

Sixth-Period Exit Ticket Answers

1. a. You should never make a change that will dramatically alter the project from what was originally proposed, even if you never have to provide follow-up data to the funder. Funders make their decisions based on your initial proposal and to dramatically change it would be unethical and potentially damaging when under consideration for future opportunities. When in doubt, check with a program officer before making any changes to ensure they are allowable.

2. *False.* Even though age is expressed as a number, it is categorical data, which means it is qualitative.

Seventh-Period Exit Ticket Answers

1. *True.* Always write a thank-you letter to keep future funding opportunities open.

2. See the list in chapter 7 about creative ways to thank and recognize a funder.

Fifty Classroom and School Grants

We have compiled a list of fifty grants available for classroom teachers, schools, and school districts. Each grant listed has a website or online webpage that will give you more details about the RFP. Just use any Internet search engine to find more information about a particular grant. Most of these grants are on an annual revolving basis, but some are rolling deadlines. Use this list to start researching and writing grants as you develop a grant-writing team at your school!

Granting organization	Title of grant or program
Active Schools Acceleration Project	ASAP Acceleration Grant
Air Force Association	Educator Grant
American Academy of Dermatology	Shade Structure Grant Program
American Association for the Advancement of Science	AAAS Leadership in Science Education Prize
American Chemical Society	Hach High School Chemistry Grant
American Honda Foundation	Grants for youth and science education
Associate of American Educators Foundation	AAEF Classroom Grant
Best Buy Children Foundation	Community grants
Build-a-Bear Workshop Bear Hugs Foundation	Literacy and Education Grant
Captain Planet Foundation	Captain Planet Foundation grants
Center for Research in Emotional and Social Health	CRESH grants
Clorox Company Foundation	Power A Bright Future program
Crayola	Champion Creatively Alive Children grants
CVS Caremark	Community grants
Dollar General Literacy Foundation	Youth Literacy grants
Dominion	Dominion K–12 Educational Partnership
Elmer's & Kids In Need Foundation	Elmer's & Kids In Need Foundation Teacher Tool Kit Grants
Ezra Keats Foundation	Ezra Jack Keats Minigrant Program
Fuel Up to Play 60	Funds for Fuel Up to Play 60

Gale/Library Media Connection	The Gale/Library Media Connection TEAMS Award
Humane Society of the United States	Humane Education Mini-Grant for Teachers
ING Financial Services	Unsung Heroes grant
KaBOOM! and Dr Pepper Snapple Group	Playground grants
Keep America Beautiful	Graffiti Hurts grant
Liberty Mutual Insurance	Responsible Sports community grant
Lois Lenski Covey Foundation, Inc.	LLCF Library Grant Program
Lowe's Charitable and Education Foundation	Lowe's Toolbox for Education grants
McCarthey Dressman Education Foundation	Academic Enrichment and Teacher Development Grants
Mr. Holland's Opus Foundation	Michael Kamen Grant Program
National Storytelling Network	Brimstone Award for Applied Storytelling
National Weather Association	Sol Hirsch Education Fund Grants
NFL Network	Keep Gym in School Grant
P. Buckley Moss Foundation for Children's Education	National Educator grants
Pioneer Drama Service	Touching Lives Through Theater Grant
Red Robin Foundation	U-ACT Grant
School Garden Network	Schoolyard Habitat Program
Snapdragon Book Foundation	Grants
Spencer Foundation	Evidence For The Classroom
Target Foundation	Field Trip Grant; Early Childhood Reading Grant
The American Institute of Aeronautics and Astronautics	AIAA Foundation Classroom Grant Program
The Herb Society of America	HSA Grant for Educators
The National Guild For Community Arts Education	MetLife Partners in Arts Education
The NEA Foundation	Student Achievement grants

The Pet Care Trust	Pets in the Classroom Teacher Grant
Toshiba America Foundation	Grants for Grades K–5 or 6–12
Urban Needs In Teacher Education (UNITE)	UNITE Classroom Grant
USA Today Charitable Foundation	USA Today Literacy Program Grant
W.K. Kellogg Foundation	W.K. Kellogg Foundation Grant
Walmart Foundation	Local, state, and national giving program
Whole Kids Foundation	School Garden Grants Program

The following flowchart depicts the entire grant-writing process.

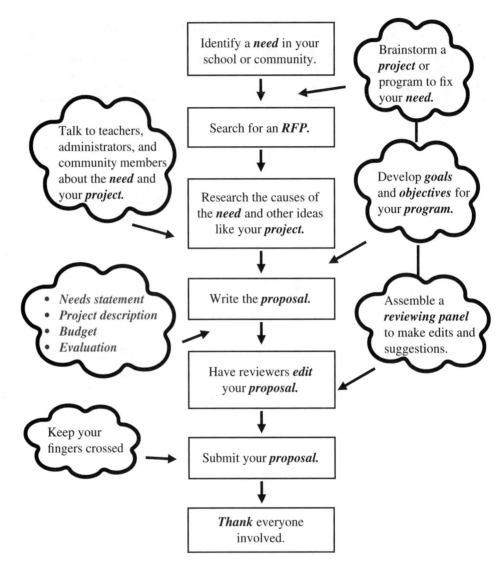

FIGURE B.1 The Grant-Writing Process

Grant-Reviewing Committee: Proposal Evaluation Rubric

This is an example of a proposal evaluation rubric that you can use to score each of the proposals based on the mock RFP found in chapter 1. Each grant-reviewing committee will have its own rubric or criteria to judge and score proposals. Put yourself in the grant-reviewing committee's shoes and score the "Operation: Eat SMART" (page 173) and "No More Desserts in the Desert" (page 178) grant proposals using the following rubric. Which proposal would you fund? How will you base your decision?

Request for Proposal: Health Awareness Evaluation Rubric

Category	Strong 10 points	Moderate 6–5 points	Below adequate 3–2 points	Nonexistent 0 points
Needs assessment	Clear explanation of a need or problem facing the students cited with at least two sources of research or documented source.	Problem or need is stated clearly, does not specifically affect students, one or no sources of research support the need.	Problem or need is not clearly stated; no credible source is mentioned that documents the need.	No problem or need is stated that affects students.
Project description	The section includes a goal or objectives, chronological project timeline, various activities that directly relate to the stated goal or objectives, and shows that the project will affect student overall health.	The section includes a goal or objectives, chronological project timeline, various activities that directly relate to the stated goal or objectives, but has a questionable impact on student overall health.	The goals or objectives listed are not aligned or are vague, activities relate to most of the objectives; direct correlation to student overall health is not evident.	No goal, objectives, or activities are listed. Student overall health will not be affected.

Teaching method	Multiple teaching or instructional methods are explained and will affect student learning, including when the teaching will occur.	Multiple teaching or instructional methods are mentioned and will affect student learning; time frame or description is vague.	Teaching or instructional methods don't directly affect student learning; time frame is listed but vague.	No teaching or instructional methods are listed.
Outcomes and evaluation	Desired outcomes are clearly stated; one or more formal evaluation tools assessing the project will be used.	Desired outcomes are clearly stated; a formal evaluation tool assessing the project is mentioned but will not yield believable data.	Desired outcomes are vague; only informal assessments are used to evaluate the project.	No outcomes are mentioned or no evaluation tool will be used.
Vision	A clear vision to expand and support the project is evident; the school and community support the vision and development in the future.	A vision to expand and support the project is included but questionable; the school and community support the vision and development in the future.	A vision to expand and support the project is included but questionable; no mention of school or community support.	No vision to expand or support the program is stated, or the vision is not believable or attainable.
Project budget	An itemized project budget is present and easy to read; each requested resource aligns to the overall goal or objectives; budget does not exceed $500.	An itemized project budget is present and easy to read; one or more requested resources do not align to overall goal or objectives; budget does not exceed $500.	An itemized project budget is not easy to follow; questionable resources are requested; budget does not exceed $500.	Budget is not itemized or exceeds $500.

TOTAL _____/60

Complete Proposal: Instructional Unit

These two proposals were written based on the mock RFP featured in chapter 1. Review the RFP from the first chapter and then see how the authors created instructional units that fit all the requirements laid out in the RFP. Look closely at each section and review the techniques and guidelines throughout this book to assess each proposal. Would you give these teachers the requested funds to implement their unit? Do the units line up with the stated objectives of the funding organization?

Operation: Eat SMART

1. *Needs assessment:* State why the funds are needed for your particular classroom. (maximum of 300 words)

> A variety of challenges are presented to my third and fourth grade students as part of everyday life in Memphis, TN, including access to physical health and wellness programs. Despite our city being ranked the most obese city in America (Centers for Disease Control and Prevention, 2010), our school recently reduced physical education by 50% and cut the already sparse health class that met once a year for six weeks.
>
> With basic health and physical education cuts, it is no wonder that the Center for Disease Control reports that child obesity has tripled in the past 30 years and that the parents of our children, mainly minority men and women, are affected the most (49.6% of African American women nationally). Education serves as the foundation for our children's future and yet a major life skill once taught has now been removed, effectively reducing the options for healthy living and increasing the likelihood of an ever-growing child obesity pandemic.
>
> The negative effects of overweight and obese children are evident in our classrooms each and every day. The daily attendance rate has methodically reduced each year, as more and more children need health care for conditions related to excessive weight. As a result of poor diets, students often come to school mentally unprepared for the day and in some cases have sugar crashes during the middle of the day from sugary drinks and snacks substituted as breakfast foods. And while our school has instituted a "Healthy School Initiative" where sugary drinks and unhealthy snacks are no longer allowed in school, it is obvious by the litter surrounding the school grounds and community that our students are making unhealthy food choices beyond the four walls of our school.

2. *Project description:* Provide a detailed description of the planned activities. How will students' overall health benefit? Include your unit or project objectives. Include a proposed timeline for the project. (maximum of 500 words)

> *Operation: Eat SMART* is a cross-curricular program developed by one third and one fourth grade teacher to replace the recently cut health class. By infusing health education and activities into each unit of curriculum, students will be exposed to healthy habits year round and begin to make SMART choices.
>
> Each unit will focus on one *SMART* strategy for weight reduction. Students will learn to eat **S**ugar-free options, **M**ove every day, **A**ssess their eating habits/options, eat **R**eal food, and **T**alk with friends and family about health.
>
> During the first quarter, students will be introduced to *Operation: Eat SMART* and address the first topic, "**S**ugar-free options." Students will learn how to read nutritional labels on the products they consume and track their dietary habits for two weeks. After recording, each grade will tabulate how much sugar they consumed over the past two weeks and visually create the total sugar consumed through a visual aid to be displayed in the school using real sugar to fill measuring cups. After discussion and lessons talking about the negative effects of having too much sugar, the third and fourth grade will then repeat the recording process for two weeks, competing against each other to see who can reduce their sugar intake.
>
> Each classroom will also implement movement into each day's lesson including teaching through kinesthetic movement and teaching about the importance of **M**oving every day. Additionally, teachers on recess duty have agreed to develop various small games to be used out at recess to keep kids active and moving during their twenty-minute recess period.
>
> During the second quarter, students will learn to **A**ssess their eating habits through using the logs from the first quarter and comparing those to suggested national and caloric guidelines provided by the USDA and CDC. Third and fourth grade teachers will also tie this to an annual food drive that takes place at this time of year. Each item collected during the school-wide food drive will be evaluated for its nutritional value and worked into sample healthy recipes that will be provided to shelters receiving the donations.
>
> The third quarter will focus on eating **R**eal food. Using their own health records and the assessments of donated food, students will begin to identify and incorporate healthy alternatives into their routines. In classrooms, students will learn about the science

behind making different tastes chemically versus the natural taste in grown foods. Additionally, the kitchen staff has agreed to run an "exchange" program where students can turn in their unhealthy snacks in return for a healthy snack. At the end of the quarter, the unhealthy snacks will be weighed to be displayed to the school and community.

Finally, in the fourth quarter, students will learn to <u>T</u>alk about healthy eating. Students will identify ways in which they have changed their habits. They will produce media campaigns outlining what they have learned that will be released by the school and local organizations, thus getting our students to become civically engaged and empowered members of their community.

Unit Timeline

Quarter #	Student activities
Quarter 1	Overview of *Operation: Eat SMART*. Classrooms will then introduce basic nutrition principles including reading of labels and review digestion. Students will also complete the sugar-reduction race.
Quarter 2	Students will chart and compare their nutritional intake and draw comparisons to recommended intakes using mixed literacy techniques. Students will also work with the school food drive to log, classify, and sort donated food items and generate healthy recipes to be sent with the foods.
Quarter 3	Students will demonstrate their mastery of mathematical skills used in calculating data including mean and median as they assess their individual records and the donated food logs. A science unit focusing on taste, the production of artificial tastes, and chemical reactions within the body caused by food will be taught to both third and fourth grade students.
Quarter 4	Students will demonstrate their cumulative knowledge by producing media campaigns focusing on healthy eating and living. Using materials already owned by the school, students will create video- or document-based information to be distributed school and community wide. Additionally, students will complete another two-week tracking to compare to the beginning of the year data.

3. *Teaching method:* Describe the teaching methods you will use to implement your project and describe how and when you will implement your project. (maximum of 150 words)

This year-long curriculum enhancement will be taught by one third and one fourth grade teacher covering a wide array of content areas including science, social science, math, literacy, and physical education. While traditional teaching methods will be employed (direct instruction, peer-to-peer, small group) this curriculum will largely rely on experiential learning with a focus on civically engaged service learning during the second quarter food drive.

Other stakeholders including cafeteria staff, recess staff, and administration will contribute to this initiative by reinforcing *Operation: Eat SMART* goals within their work. Upon conclusion, the community at large will be provided an opportunity to engage in student learning through the production and distribution of the students' media campaigns.

4. *Outcomes and evaluation:* Describe the expected outcomes and evaluation methods you will use to measure your project's success. Be specific. (maximum of 300 words)

Data will be collected intermittently to check for progress and inform immediate plans. Additionally, a final assessment will be provided to capture both formative and summative information. Specific outcomes are as follows:

1. Students will demonstrate a mastery of knowledge regarding reading nutritional labels.

2. Students will effectively be able to compare and draw conclusions regarding different food options available to them.

3. 90% of third and fourth grade students will reduce their sugar intake from quarter 1 to quarter 4 by no less than 25%.

4. Students' self-efficacy regarding their ability to talk about food options will increase in a statistically significant manner.

Pre- and post-assessments will be used to measure the above items. Other measurable outcomes include the sugar reduction race, activity time at recess, healthy snack exchange program, and media campaign projects. These data points will be used as qualitative measurements to supplement the above quantitative measures.

Other assessments will also be provided throughout various science, social science, math, and literacy classrooms as this curriculum enhancement will be part of the graded portion of students work.

5. *Vision:* Describe your vision and plan for replicating or adapting your project within your school or district. (maximum of 150 words)

The school administration has shown support for this project by engaging school staff beyond the third and fourth grade teachers in the implementation plan and by allocating some school resources including video cameras, paper goods, and planning time. Once the project is proven successful, we will begin adding one grade level per year to better infuse the curriculum and make certain programs (sugar reduction race and healthy exchange) school wide.

Last, local community organizations, which are engaged during the dissemination of media campaigns, will use their resources to supplement existing school resources to sustain and replicate this project not only within our school, but also in other schools citywide. Once such organization that has stepped forward is the Memphis Chamber of Commerce, who plans to tie this school initiative to their small business incubation program for low-income communities within and around Memphis.

6. *Project budget:* List materials, equipment costs, etc. needed to implement your project. List each item separately. Provide a total amount for all expenses.

Materials, equipment, resources	Number of units	Cost per unit	Cost
Nutritional recording books—produced in-house	70	$3.50	$245.00
Sugar—20 five-pound bags	20	$7.50	$150.00
Colored duct tape multipack—recess games	3	$2.37	$7.11
White copy paper pack	3	$17.00	$51.00
Shipping	1	$21.73	$21.73
Total Requested			**$474.84**

Note: All products will be purchased with six months of award to conform to Health Awareness Classroom guidelines.

The following resources will be provided at no charge to the grant:

Materials, equipment, resources	Number of units	Cost per unit	Cost
Measuring cups and glasses	100	$3.99	$399.00
Flip Video Cameras—previously owned for 1 year (depreciated value shown)	6	$120.00	$720.00
Healthy snacks for exchange program provided by cafeteria—estimated 150 snacks exchanged @ $.74/snack	150	$.74	$111.00
Community organizers time—calculated at 5 hrs @ $23/hour for 3 organizers			$345.00
Total in-kind match			**$1,575.00**

No More Desserts in the Desert

1. *Needs assessment:* State why the funds are needed for your particular classroom. (maximum of 300 words)

> The majority of my 7th grade students live in one of the designated "food deserts" in downtown Atlanta, Georgia, according to the USDA's Food Desert Locator (name recently changed to the Food Access Research Atlas). A food desert is a populated area that is void of fresh food options up to a one-mile radius (USDA, 2010). My students constantly arrive to school with bags of chips, candy bars, fruit cocktail juice mixes high in sugar, and soda. When asked about their unhealthy purchases, my students respond that there are no healthy options for snacks on their way to school. According to a recent study by the Atlanta Regional Commission, only half of low-income families in the Atlanta city limits have equal access to fresh food in relation to fast food. According to the US Centers for Disease Control and Prevention, "limited access to nutritious food and relatively easier access to less nutritious food may be linked to poor diets and, ultimately, to obesity and diet-related diseases."

> Student nutrition and diet have been tied to academic performance in a number of studies, including the Children's Lifestyle and School-performance Study. The results of this study found that "students with decreased overall diet quality were significantly more likely to perform poorly" on a given assessment and on school academics (Florence, 2008). Without knowledge of the effects of their eating habits and raising awareness about the need for fresh food in their community, the majority of my students will continue to suffer from a non-nutritious diet and decreased academic performance.

2. *Project description:* Provide a detailed description of the planned activities. How will students' overall health benefit? Include your unit or project objectives. Include a proposed timeline for the project. (maximum of 500 words)

> The title of my proposed combination science and social studies classroom unit is "No More Desserts in the Desert." My 7th grade students will investigate the nutritious value, or lack thereof, in their daily diet and raise awareness about the lack of healthy food options in the downtown Atlanta district. These learning outcomes will be stated in two distinct yet related objectives: (1) students will be able to use labeled nutritional value facts to assess the nutrition of their daily food choices and (2) students will propose a tangible solution to raising awareness about the need for healthy food options in their community.

> The week before I begin the actual unit, I will have my students document the nutrition facts for all food and drinks they consume

for five consecutive days. This will be introduced only as a homework assignment. The students will then use this documentation the following week to analyze their nutritional value intake when the actual unit begins. Other activities will include lessons on assessing nutritional value, the difference between saturated and unsaturated fats, the carbohydrate energy cycle, and the importance of the body receiving the right amount of each daily vitamin. Students will then conduct a mini-research project on a disease of illness that is caused by an unhealthy diet. Students will then create a weekly menu of healthy food items and balance a weekly nutritional fact sheet. Finally students will assess the available food options in their community, plot healthy and non-healthy food options on a map, and raise awareness about the lack of healthy food options in their community.

Students' overall health will benefit by bringing to light the lack of nutrition they are currently consuming, creating a healthy menu, and finding the closest healthy food option in their community.

Unit Timeline

Week number	Student activities
Week leading up to unit	Students document the nutrition facts of food and drink items for five consecutive days.
Weeks 1–2	Science lesson on assessing nutrition value, essentials to a healthy diet, difference between saturated and unsaturated fats, the carbohydrate energy cycle, and the importance of the body receiving the right amount of each daily vitamin.
Week 3	Research project and presentation on a disease or illness caused by unhealthy diet. Students also create a healthy meal menu and balance the nutrition values.
Weeks 4–5	Students will plot the valuable food options in their community, create a poster, radio advertisement, or short commercial about the lack of healthy food options.
Week 6	Students document their eating habits using their healthy menu and balanced nutrition chart.

3. *Teaching method:* Describe the teaching methods you will use to implement your project and describe how and when you will implement your project. (maximum of 150 words)

A variety of instructional methods will be used throughout the unit, including direct instruction, peer-to-peer instruction, small-group research teams, project-based learning, and inquiry-based learning. This variance in instructional methods will ensure that all learners will receive instruction through various means catered to individual learning styles. Differentiation will be a driving component of each type of instruction to ensure that each student is challenged at his or her ability level.

The project will take place during the first six weeks of the second quarter of the academic year, roughly beginning of October up until mid-November.

4. *Outcomes and evaluation:* Describe the expected outcomes and evaluation methods you will use to measure your project's success. Be specific. (maximum of 300 words)

This unit's success will be evaluated multiple times throughout the unit. The formal summative evaluation tool will be twofold. Students will measure the change in their eating habits from their pre-unit documentation and post-unit documentation of their daily food intake. Students will also take a pre-test and post-test assessing their content knowledge of both the science and social studies standards covered during this unit (i.e., nutritional terms and geographical mapping skills).

Students' progress will be informally measured through daily exit tickets, a research project based on an illness related to diet, the mapping of food options in the community, and the community awareness portion of the unit.

I expect 90% of students to increase their scores from the pre to post standards based assessment and 75% of students to improve their diet based on their post-unit diet documentation.

5. *Vision:* Describe your vision and plan for replicating or adapting your project within your school or district. (maximum of 150 words)

Upon this unit's success, I plan to approach the Truly Living Well Wheat Street Garden, a nonprofit organization, that turned a once-dilapidated housing project into a four-acre urban garden providing fresh fruits and vegetables to the citizen of inner city Atlanta. I hope to secure a partnership between our school and the TLW Wheat Street Garden in which in each subsequent year all 7th grade science and social studies classrooms at our school can visit the urban garden, study the impact of the garden on Atlanta, and help to raise funds to increase the TLW Wheat Street Garden mission. This will become the community outreach component of future units and will ensure the stability of funding and community support to continue the "No More Desserts in the Desert" unit.

6. *Project budget:* List materials, equipment costs, etc. needed to implement your project. List each item separately. Provide a total amount for all expenses.

Materials, equipment, resources	Number of units	Cost per unit	Cost
Map of Atlanta	12	$3	$36
Chart paper	2	$27	$54
Construction colored paper pack	1	$22	$22
White copy paper pack	1	$17	$17
Carbohydrate experiment materials	1	$46	$46
Food and Nutrition for Every Kid	1	$11.98	$11.98
Diet Minder Food and Exercise Journal For Kids	30	$9.86	$295.80
The Mayo Clinic Kids Cookbook	1	$15.96	$15.96
Total Requested			**$489.74**

Example of a Classroom Instructional Unit Grant

The following proposal was submitted by Katie Lyons, a veteran middle school language arts teacher. This proposal was written in 2011 and was fully funded by the Chicago Foundation for Education, a foundation that supports teachers in Chicago Public Schools. The Chicago Foundation for Education supports more than one thousand teachers each year through various classroom, leadership, research, and team member study grants. Katie Lyons's proposed unit was entitled "From Tupac to Tennyson: A Spoken-Word Poetry Revolution" and was written for her middle school language arts classroom.

1. Describe your project and the key activities included.

> In this interactive, performance-based unit on the spoken word, students will compare classic poetry to the contemporary hip-hop poets and rappers of today. Students will learn about the roots of poetry as an oral tradition and analyze how the evolution of spoken-word poetry moved from the Beats to rap and hip-hop to performance art. In addition to analyzing Shakespearean sonnets, students will also interpret lyrics from musical artists such as Tupac. Through close examinations of the written and spoken word, students will analyze poetic literary devices (such as symbolism, imagery, metaphor) and apply their understandings of the devices by composing and performing their own poems. Furthermore, students will use technology to record their composed poems and then transform their recordings into video productions to be showcased at a schoolwide poetry slam.

The key activities are described in detail and will definitely engage students and add to student learning. The author could have used a more focused approach to outlining the project, including stating an explicit objective or objectives. The author mentions three possible learning statements that could be considered the objectives (compare classic poetry to the contemporary hip-hop poets and rappers, learn about the roots of poetry as an oral tradition, analyze the evolution of spoken-word poetry). When describing your project, be very specific about the desired outcomes, for example, "At the completion of this unit, students will be able to . . . "

2. Please explain why the materials and resources outlined in your budget are necessary to complete the project.

> The resources will aid in developing an interactive poetry unit that incorporates students' interests (rap and music videos) while not neglecting the importance of influential poets such as Langston Hughes. Students will analyze poems; listen to audios of the poets to learn how to create spoken word; and manipulate the flip cameras to record themselves reciting their poems. Also, the resources will support a trip to the Apple store to transform the recorded poems into multimedia presentations.

> *The author's proposed trip to the Apple store is a component that sets her proposal apart from a standard instructional unit grant application. This unique experience will allow students to travel out of the building and learn from an expert in the field. The students will be learning twenty-first-century technology skills and applying the skills directly to their created work! Refer to chapter 3 for more ideas about how to strengthen your proposal!*

3. Describe the specific learning needs and the Illinois Learning Standards that are being addressed by this project.

> The activities will engage students in analyzing how poets use the written and spoken word to express ideas. Students will examine how poets use metaphoric and figurative language as well as poetic devices (alliteration, rhyme scheme, unrhymed verse) to convey meaning. Students will learn about the important themes and perspectives that emerged during the different poets' lifetimes and they will use this knowledge to interpret the poets' point of view. Students will apply their knowledge of the written and spoken poetic language to compose their own poems that reflect their unique experience as a black child growing up in the 21st century. Students will synthesize their analysis of current political events and reflect on the challenges of their lives growing up as pre-teens in the Chicago housing projects through the composition of their poems. Students will enhance their creative writing and performance skills through the production of a multimedia video presentation.

4. What formal and informal learning tools will you use to evaluate how your project increases student learning?

> Students will write a reflection of each poet's work analyzing the language the poet used to express his/her perspective. Students will compose a poem that reflects their experiences growing up in today's society. Students will then write an essay elaborating on how their poem illustrates their life experiences and relates to current events. Students will record themselves reciting their poem and they will then create a multimedia video presentation of their poem.

Make sure to state which learning tools are formal and which are informal. Your response should directly answer the question prompt. If the prompt asks for formal-informal or summative-formative, make sure you specifically label each learning tool or assessment as one of the categories mentioned in the prompt. Don't forget to mention how each learning tool or assessment will help you evaluate the project's overall impact on student learning. The author here could have included how she will measure the increase in student learning by use of a formal assessment. A pre- and posttest evaluating the students' knowledge of symbolism, imagery, and metaphor (as previously mentioned) in poetry could be used to measure student learning in relation to a stated objective or standard.

5. Itemize your budget requests; include all materials, equipment, and tentative sources of supplies along with the cost of each item. Your budget may not exceed $500. Please note that money cannot be used to pay CPS district personnel and should NOT include sales tax. Round costs to the nearest dollar.

Hip-Hop Poetry and The Classics, by Alan Lawrence Sitomer and Michael Cirelli	Amazon	$20.00
Poetry for Young People: Langston Hughes, edited by David Roessel	Amazon	$15.00
Hip Hop Speaks to Children with CD: A Celebration of Poetry with a Beat (A Poetry Speaks Experience), by Nikki Giovanni	Amazon	$20.00

Oxford Book of American Poetry, by David Lehman and John Brehm	Amazon	$30.00
Stage a Poetry Slam: Creating Performance Poetry Events: Inside Tips, Backstage Advice and Lots of Examples, by Marc Kelly Smith and Joe Kraynak	Amazon	$15.00
Flip video camera, Ultra HD 8 GB	Flip video	$200.00
Bus transportation from school to Apple store on Michigan Ave.	Sunrise Bus Company	$180.00
The Rose That Grew from Concrete, by Tupac Shakur	Amazon	$20.00
Total		$500.00

The budget is itemized but not easy to read. Although each requested resource is explained in context in the proposal, the individual line items appear cluttered. The author should have formatted the book titles in a manner easier for viewing such as an APA or MLA format. For aesthetic viewing purposes, it may be beneficial to group the resources by one category (i.e., materials, equipment, etc.). Another method would be to sort like items together such as all books together. Additionally, because the instructions request rounded dollar figures, there is no need to list values in the above format showing zero cents. Instead, simply show dollar figures for each item as a whole number amount such as, "Flip video camera, Ultra HD 8GB—$200."

Example of a Teacher Travel Grant

The following proposal was submitted by John Dudley, a veteran high school history teacher. This proposal was written in 2008 and was fully funded. John Dudley and another colleague were able to complete their entire proposed travel project with the awarded funding. An excerpt of this proposal also appears in chapter 3.

Project description: Please describe your project in detail and outline each phase of travel.

> My colleague and I are interested in pursuing a fellowship in South Africa. The overall theme for this two-week in-depth examination will be diversity and change. We will further subdivide this theme into three specific objectives or areas of study: diversity in culture and expression, diversity in flora and fauna, and historic change and the legacy of apartheid.

The overarching goal, stated here as "overall theme," appears at the very beginning of the project description, which creates a focus for the entire section. The theme is then broken down into three tangible objectives or areas of study. This focus follows the discussion of creating goals and objectives as described in chapter 3. A strong project description will make sure to describe how each of these objectives will be achieved in relation to the overall goal.

> South Africa has an amazingly diverse population, with 11 different national languages. In completing this fellowship our first goal is to engage the people of this unique nation. We have no prejudices, whether they be white, black, rich, or poor, we want to hear about their lives and their experiences in South Africa. We will do this through conversation, participating in local events and celebrations, and through township home-stays (a township is an area of land, generally on the outskirts of South Africa's major cities, that was reserved for non-whites during the Apartheid era. Townships generally are composed of poor blacks and shoddy housing). We will also examine the public schools in various parts of the country to make comparisons between our education system and theirs. And we will also view the artwork of the township people of South Africa, in the hopes of viewing the world, and their country, and their lives, through their eyes.
>
> It has only been 16 years since Nelson Mandela was released from the Robben Island prison which held him for nearly 3 decades.

And it has only been 12 years since South Africa held its first democratic election. The nation is still changing, and recovering, and recoiling from the almost 50 years of Apartheid rule. Our third goal in traveling to South Africa is to examine the legacy of Apartheid and in particular its impact on the native black community. We will do this through historic examination, visiting the one-time home of Nelson Mandela in Soweto, traveling by boat to Robben Island to see the prison which shackled him for so long, and visiting the Apartheid Museum in Johannesburg, and the Mandela museum in Umtata. Furthermore we will look at the other important figures of the Anti-Apartheid movement including Steve Biko, Desmond Tutu, and Hector Pieterson (whose death sparked a 2-year uprising in Soweto). We will also achieve our goal through direct, but respectful, conversation with South Africans of every color. In particular, however, we plan to spend time in the poor townships discussing the Apartheid era, and the successes and failures of the South African government, now that the majority black population is in charge.

In order to successfully complete these three objectives we will travel in a circuit route through the heart of South Africa. We will begin in Cape Town on the country's southwest coast. Cape Town is the oldest South African city (still in existence), and due to its natural beauty, it also happens to be a cultural melting pot of Africans, white Europeans, indigenous tribal peoples, and, of course, tourists. We will stay in Cape Town for 6 days. During our time there we will visit Robben Island prison (where Nelson Mandela was held) and the District 6 museum (District 6 was a successfully integrated community in Cape Town that housed both black and white families for 100 years. It was considered a cultural center until 1966 when the Nationalist government declared District 6 a "white-area" and forcibly removed the community's 60,000 black residents). In an effort to immerse ourselves in South Africa's culture we will spend a day and a half in Cape Town's largest township, Khayelisthsa, where we will meet with locals, tour the housing, visit schools, and dine in one of the small township eateries. We will stay for the night at a small inn in the township, and then travel the next morning, by rental car, to the Cape of Good Hope Nature Reserve, one of the country's largest displays of its unique flora and fauna.

On the 6th day of our stay we will fly by commercial plane 1,000 miles east of Cape Town to Johannesburg, the largest city in South Africa. We will spend only 2 days in Johannesburg, enough time to take in the "Tried for Treason" Mandela exhibit at the Africa Museum, and to visit the highly recommended Apartheid

Museum. Following our 2nd night in Johannesburg we will take a bus out to that city's main township, Soweto. Soweto is the largest township in South Africa, and contains the only street in the world where two Nobel Peace Prize winners lived, Nelson Mandela and Desmond Tutu. It also has the largest township art gallery in South Africa, the Soweto Art Gallery. In furthering our cultural and historical studies we plan to spend the night in Soweto on a home-stay, an arrangement through one of the township touring companies where travelers can stay the night with a local black family.

Following our night in Soweto we will travel by bus 300 miles southeast to Durban, a large industrial city sitting on the western edge of the Indian Ocean. Our stay in Durban, like in Johannesburg, will only be for 2 days. We hope there to continue our cultural conversations with local South Africans, and to visit some of the nation's public schools. Furthermore we will visit the BAT Centre, one of South Africa's largest performance and display art venues. At the BAT Centre we will examine more of the nation's self-expression through art, and take in an evening dance performance.

Leaving out of Durban we will take a traveler's bus 250 miles west to Umtata, the hometown of Nelson Mandela, and the current location of the Mandela Museum. We will spend half of the day there, and the other half in King William's Town, 120 miles further west. King William's Town is the birthplace and final resting place of Steven Biko, founder of the Black Consciousness movement, and a legendary hero of the Anti-Apartheid movement. Continuing on, on our way back west toward Cape Town, we will spend a day in East London, meeting with locals and visiting schools. In East London we will also rent a car, with the intention of driving the remaining 600 miles to Cape Town along the southern coast of South Africa, a route known as the Garden Route, naturally because of its incomparable landscape, wildlife, and environmental beauty.

On the first day of our drive out of East London we will drive about 120 miles west, before detouring north to visit the Addo Elephant Park: a game reserve containing various animal and plant species, including giraffes, lions, leopards, black rhinos, and, of course, elephants. We will travel from there another 20 miles north to the Mountain Zebra reserve where we will rent a cabin for the night. In the morning we will continue our examination of the flora and fauna of South Africa with a tour of the Mountain Zebra reserve itself. In the afternoon we will drive 350 miles west to the DeHoop Nature Reserve, stopping along the way at areas of interest, and to examine the unique landscape of the Garden

Route. At DeHoop we will rent another cabin for our last night in South Africa, and in the morning we will drive the remaining 130 miles to Cape Town for our flight home to the United States.

Benefits to teacher: Please describe the benefits to each teacher participating in the project. How will the overall travel experience impact the teacher's instruction?

The impulse for this project is that we teach in an embattled inner-city community. Our students are all black, and the community that surrounds the school is 98 percent African American. My colleague and I are both white and we struggle to find common ground with the families who send their children to our school. Obviously as Americans and as stakeholders in the future lives of their students we have a connection, but otherwise there is a clear cultural gap between us and this community. We believe that we can bridge this gap, however, by immersing ourselves in the root culture of African peoples, and by determining for ourselves the inspiration and inherent motives that inspire black communities back home.

> *The author is able to provide a short needs statement within the proposal under a different prompt. This is a great strategy to create a connection between the grant-reviewing panel and your targeted audience when there is no specific needs statement section given within an RFP.*

Furthermore this experience will help us grow as teachers in that we will discover our own ability to share our native culture with those whom we visit, as well as the ability to listen and draw from the experiences of the South African people. That exchange will benefit our teaching practice because it will help us to determine which aspects of our culture are unique and important and should be taught, and which aspects are more trivial, self-aggrandizing, and are better off ignored. Furthermore, in spending an extended period of time in South Africa we will be able to visit schools, talk to students, and teachers, and learn about the education system of another country, in particular an African one. Obviously the insights that we gain from that experience will have a profound impact on how we teach and interact with our students when we return to America.

To put ourselves out there and to share our experiences and to critically examine how another part of the world lives, and in particular how it educates its people, and tries to (or doesn't try to) help its impoverished communities, is an important effort that will forever impact and influence our lives. We are both passionate about learning, and we are both extremely passionate about our students and the work that we do with them. We feel that this experience will make us better teachers because we will have diversified our understanding of African culture, the struggles and successes of poor communities, and the nature of people to teach each other and to learn from one another, regardless of race and homeland.

Benefits to students: Please describe the benefits to the students of the teacher participating in the project. How will the overall travel experience impact students?

In the community we teach our students have been, for the most part, disenfranchised from the American Dream. They face monumental challenges on a daily basis, are behind in their education, and have a hard time getting help from the politicians they elect and the media outlets that judge them. Our students need to see a community like theirs that has successfully stood up for itself, and implemented a system of change. In this regard we chose South Africa because of its recent overthrow of Apartheid oppression. Our students need to see that injustice is not omnipotent, and that change can come from grassroots community movements that act in the name of righteousness. We will therefore collect artifacts and record stories from the Apartheid era. We will bring back pictures, and maps, and charts, and personal accounts of violence, struggle, and victory. We will demonstrate for our students visually, sensually, and through writing how one embattled community of Africans overcame their oppressors and successfully took control of their government.

Furthermore this experience will help augment our students' learning in that they will discover how young people live and are educated in South Africa. Ideally we will be able to do this by establishing a partnership with a high school–level institution in Cape Town or Durban, so that our students can develop a system of correspondence (whether through e-mail, teleconference, or handwritten letters) with the students whom we meet there. In this way they will be able to engage in active discussion about their lives and the lives of the South African students, allowing us to bring our experience to our students, and allowing them to make it their own.

Benefits to school: Please describe the benefits to the entire school of the teacher participating in the project. How will the overall travel experience impact the entire school community?

Upon return we will begin the year by establishing a display in the library of our artifacts, maps, pictures, and written accounts of our experience. Furthermore we will hold a professional development seminar at the start of the year to discuss three skills we expect to develop. Those skills are creating an educational travel itinerary (so that future members of our school can create and apply for their own travel grant); cultural immersion activities (including how to learn about local customs, engage locals in conversation, and how to document cultural experiences, sacred or common); and last, forming partnerships with educational institutions in foreign countries. It is our hope that the partnership we form with a South African school will be available to all of the teachers at our high school. So that if one of our math teachers wants to discuss strategies with a Cape Town geometry teacher he can. Or if our principal is curious as to how a South African school teaches reading he has an authentic, available resource to utilize. This exchange would not only benefit our high school, but also the school in South Africa that agrees to work with us. Ideally it will open a gateway for not only the exchange of information, but perhaps even the exchange of teachers for a limited time, and likewise, possibly even students, or a team of teachers and students.

Documentation: Please describe how each phase of the project will be documented and shared with stakeholders.

This is another method of asking for an assessment plan. Because this grant is specific to teacher development through travel, it would be difficult to assess a teacher's growth. Instead, the funder is asking for a documentation plan but the premise is still the same. The author does an excellent job by covering a number of methods that will reach a wide audience.

We plan to use several different forms of documentation to report on our experience. We will of course use artifacts that we collect from our travel, including clothing, masks, tools, jewelry, posters, maps, and relics of Apartheid. Furthermore, we will document our experience through a weblog. A weblog is an information board on the Internet that can be created to provide stories, journal entries, editorials, and photographs for people who are curious about the experience. Speaking of photographs, my colleague and I both have digital cameras, and we plan on taking a numerous amount of photographs (shooting people only upon permission, as of course is the African tradition), which we will display on the weblog, and on a massive collage in the school's library. Between the artifacts, the library display, and the weblog, curious information seekers will have plenty of opportunity to explore, discover, and interact with our experience in South Africa.

Budget: Please provide a line item–based budget with all expenses for your trip based on your travel description. The maximum amount requested cannot exceed $10,000.

Line item	Category	Estimated amount
Two roundtrip airplane tickets on South Africa Airlines	Travel	$4,600.00
Nine nights' stay at hostel/low-budget hotels in various locales	Accommodations	$400.00
Two nights stay in township accommodations, including home stays	Accommodations	$100.00
Two nights stay in natural game reserve cabins	Accommodations	$100.00
Fourteen days of food costs at a rate of $50 per day	Food	$700.00
Rental car for trip from Cape Town to the Cape Nature Reserve (w/gas)	Travel	$45.00
Rental car for trip from East London to Cape Town (w/gas)	Travel	$200.00
Two one-way airplane tickets from Cape Town to Johannesburg	Travel	$255.00
Bus travel from Johannesburg to Durban on Baz Bus company service	Travel	$100.00
Bus travel from Durban to East London (via Umtata and KWTown)	Travel	$100.00
Boat and tour of Robben Island Prison in Cape Town	Travel	$40.00
Museum entrance fees, area specific tours, and exhibits	Educational	$100.00

Entrance fees to natural reserves and game reserves	Educational	$60.00
Reference materials and supplies for trip to South Africa	Travel	$100.00
Misc. educational souvenirs, artifacts, relics, etc. for display and either personal or school use	Educational	$300.00
Total:		**$7,200.00**

The budget meets the minimum requirements with ease; it is not over budget, it is line-item based, and is simple enough to follow. The author adds a "category" column to assist the reviewer with the evaluation of how grant funds are going to be spent. Although a "quantity" column could be used, in this context (because not many physical items are to be purchased) it is okay to do without.

Example of a Final Report of a Grant-Supported Program

Figure B.2 shows an excerpt from the final report submitted to partner funders of UNITE's summer program GET SCIENCE! during its pilot year in 2012. Refer to chapter 7 for information about communicating results with partners and the funding organizations. Notice how this report combines data, charts, pictures, and text to create an easy-to-follow yet detailed report about student scores, financials, and thanking those involved. To download the complete GET SCIENCE! final program report in color, visit the resource page associated with this book at Wiley.com and www.urbanneeds.org/Insiders_Guide .html.

4

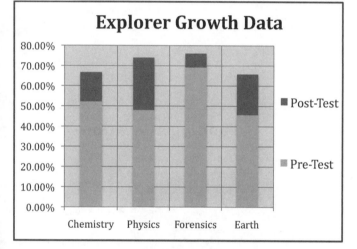

Explorer Data

We love Science!

During the **four** week summer science camp, Explorers spent one week investigating and learning about each of the following sciences: Chemistry, **Physics**, Forensics, and **Earth Science**. The Explorers took a pre-assessment in each science on Monday of every week and a post-assessment at the end of the week. Explorers' average scores increased in all of the four sciences! NCEs value added instruction is shown on the graph below. Wow, Physics! 26% increase in Explorer scores in just one week of instruction!

Explorers are all students from Chicago Public Schools attending schools on the Westside of Chicago.

Daily Schedule
8:00-8:15am   **Breakfast**
8:15-11:00am   **Science Instruction**
11:00-11:30am   **Lunch**
11:30- 1:30pm   **Science Inquiry**
1:30-2:30pm   **Girl Empowerment**

Explorer Growth Data

(bar chart showing Pre-Test and Post-Test percentages for Chemistry, Physics, Forensics, and Earth; y-axis from 0.00% to 80.00%)

- Post-Test
- Pre-Test

Can you use Forensics to solve the mystery?

CUIDADO   CAUTION   CUIDADO

At the conclusion of the GET SCIENCE! day, Explorers joined together for their one-hour Girl Empowerment session. The Explorers talked about issues such as **self-esteem**, **conflict resolution**, self-worth, **appearance**, female stereotypes, and media influences. A facilitator from the **American Red Cross** also visited the Explorers twice during the summer to speak about first aid basics and home safety procedures.

Alternatives, Inc., a non profit organization in Chicago, visited during professional development to model girl empowerment sessions for the NCEs. The NCEs worked together to create a dynamic and informative girl empowerment curriculum to meet the **emotional needs** of female students entering third through sixth grade.

For questions regarding data gathered or displayed, please contact UNITE at unite@urbanneeds.org.

"G-E-T! S-C-I-E-N-C-E! I am a girl and science is for me!"

FIGURE B.2 GET SCIENCE! Program Report (Partial)

5

A huge "thank you" to all of our partners who made this summer program possible!

Henson Elementary School
Steans Family Foundation
Chicago Public Schools
Chicago Teacher Education Pipeline™
American Red Cross
Alternatives, Inc.
Museum of Science and Industry
Open Books Literacy Center

Professional Development Presenters

Eric Snodgrass Professor, University of Illinois
Dr. Linda Figgins Professor, Illinois State University

NCE University Affiliations

Illinois State University
Concordia University
Michigan State University
Loyola University

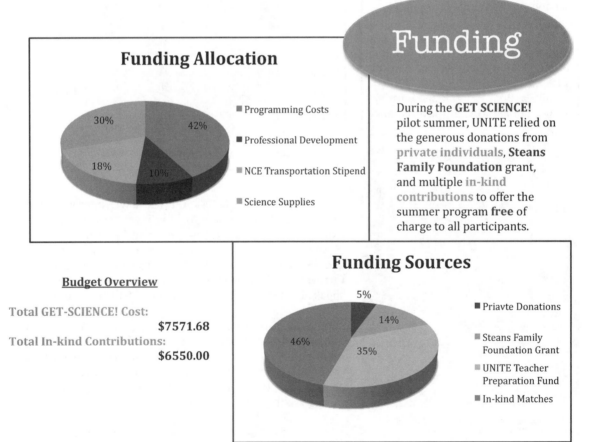

Funding Allocation

- Programming Costs
- Professional Development
- NCE Transportation Stipend
- Science Supplies

42%
30%
18%
10%

Funding

During the **GET SCIENCE!** pilot summer, UNITE relied on the generous donations from private individuals, **Steans Family Foundation** grant, and multiple in-kind contributions to offer the summer program **free** of charge to all participants.

Budget Overview

Total GET-SCIENCE! Cost:
$7571.68
Total In-kind Contributions:
$6550.00

Funding Sources

- Priavte Donations
- Steans Family Foundation Grant
- UNITE Teacher Preparation Fund
- In-kind Matches

5%
14%
35%
46%

FIGURE B.2 (Continued)

Index

A

Academics: data collection of, 117–118; development in, 58, 102, 146; games in, 29

Acronyms, 57

Active writing style, 24

Adjectives, 28–30

Adjustments, 120–122

After-school program, 133

Alignment, 48–49

American Honda Foundation, 3

Analysis, 122; grant application, 9–16

Anecdotal evidence, 29; in needs statement, 41–43

Anonymity, 116–117

Answer worksheet: budget, 157–158; ledger activity, 159–160; needs statement, 155–156; Word count I and II, 153–154

Application, 6–7, 8; analyzing, 9–16; follow-up, 136; without needs statement, 43–44

Assessment and evaluation, 34, 109–110; plan, 112–115, 132

Assessment process, 110–111; adjustments, 120–122; analysis, 122; assessment plan building, 112–115, 132; data collection, 115–120; report findings, 122–125. *See also* Needs assessment

Association of American Educators Classroom Grant RFP, 59–60

Audience, 109, 123

Author (you), 69; assessment of, 109–110; interests, 123; needs, 122

"Award amount" section, 10

Award letter, 130–132

B

Basics, 53–54

Benefits: to school, 190–191; to students, 190; to teacher, 189–190

Bill and Melinda Gates Foundation, 4

Budget, 34, 67–69; advanced techniques, 85–89; answer worksheet, 157–158; category column, 185, 193; consumables, 86–87; Eat SMART, 177; in evaluation rubric, 172; hiring personnel, 87–88; identifying what to buy, 71–75; indirect costs, 88–89; invoice, 93; itemized, 184–185; narrative, 68; No More Desserts in the Desert, 181; prompts, 75–79; teacher travel grant, 192–193; timeline, 68; From Tupac to Tennyson: A Spoken-Word Poetry Revolution, 182–183, 184–185; viewing, 184–185; worksheet, 149

Budget presentation: descriptions, 80; formatting, 82–83; funder outline for, 79; identifying features, 80; product number, 81; quantity, 80; shipping, 81; simplicity, 84–85; total cost (line), 81; total cost (project), 81; unit cost, 81

Business support, 6

C

Character count, 31–33, 52

Checklist, 19–20; needs statement, 141–142, 148, 155–156

Checkmate, 61–63

Check-Mates, 63–64

Checkout system, 101

Checkpoint, 102–104

Chicago Foundation for Education, 5, 182

Chicago Teacher Education Pipeline, 141

Collaboration, 108

Common knowledge, 30

Communication, 127; award letter, 130–132; follow-up, 134; ongoing, 132–134; rejection letter, 128–130; with stakeholders, 130

Community: engagement data collection, 120; follow-up communication to school, 134; local foundation, 5

Composition: tools checklist, 19–20; writing style, 20–31

Consistency, 52; in writing style, 30–31

Consumables budget, 86–87

"Contact information" section, 12

Contractual items, 73

Conversational writing style, 20–22

Copies, 128

Corporate foundation, 5

Credit account, 95

Cruise, Tom, 2

Culture and climate data collection, 119

Curriculum enhancement, 1

D

Danielson Framework for Teaching, 117

Data: anonymity and, 116–117; citing, 109; collection, 115–120; demographic, 108; to include in needs statement, 40–41; qualitative, 113–115; quantitative, 113–115; research and, 30; types, 115

Debit account, 95

Dedicated account approach, 94

Demographic data, 108

Department approach, 94

Department of Education (DOE), 6

"Description or purpose of grant program" section, 10. *See also* Project or program description

Districtwide program, 133

Documentation: plan, 191–192; procedures, 99–100

DOE. *See* Department of Education

Dollar General Literacy Foundation, 3

Donor's Choose, 5–6, 73

Dudley, John, 186–193

E

Eat SMART, 173–177

Economics. *See* Budget; Matching; Money management

Editing, 125; symbols, 144, 146; team, 33

Employee identification number (EIN), 9

End-of-year report, 133

English teachers, 28

Equipment purchasing, 72–73

Evaluation, 15, 124; Eat SMART, 176; learning, 183–184; No More Desserts in the Desert, 180; pre- and posttest, 184; of project description, 58; rubric, 13, 171–172. *See also* Assessment and evaluation

Evidence based writing style, 28–30

Exit ticket: answers, 165–166; first period, 18, 165; second period, 35, 165; third period, 65, 165; fourth period, 92, 165–166; fifth period, 105, 166; sixth period, 126, 166; seventh period, 137, 166

Expenditures, 69

Extended classroom project or unit, 132–133

External users: assessment of, 110; interests of, 124; needs, 123

Extracurricular activities, 1; after-school programs, 133

Ezra Jack Keats Minigrant Program, 51, 60

F

Facebook, 8

Factual writing style, 25–27

Family foundations, 4

Final report, 194–196

Financial reporting, 95–96, 103

First–person writing style, 22–24

Fiscal agent, 94–95

Fiscal calendars, 102

Five Ws and how. *See* Who, what, where, when, why, and how

501(c)3 organizations, 5–6, 9

Follow-up: applications, 136; communication, 134; rejection letter, 129–130

Formal learning tools, 184

Foundation Center, 7

Foundations, 4–6. *See also specific foundations*

From Tupac to Tennyson: A Spoken-Word Poetry Revolution, 182–185

Funder: assessment of, 110; budget outline, 79; follow-up communication to, 134; interests, 123–124; needs, 122–123; new, 136; relationship building with, 135–136

Funding organization, 2, 9; in media releases, 134

Future, 136–137

G

Generally accepted accounting principles (GAAP), 97

Geographic area, 7

GET SCIENCE! (Girl Empowerment Through Science Camp with Integrating the Enhancement of Newly Certified Educators), 57; final report, 194–196

Goals: as identified in planning template, 139; objectives *versus*, 48–50; in RFP, 51; teacher travel grant, 186; writing, 47–50

Gooding, Cuba, Jr., 2

Government grants, 6

Grant: available for teachers and schools, 167–169; government, 6; instructional unit, 182–185; matching, 77, 90–92; one-time award, 3, 161; prompt, 118; revolving deadline, 3, 161; rolling deadline, 2–3, 161; teacher travel, 186–193; types of, 2–3. *See also specific types of grants*

Grant application. *See* Application

Granting organizations, 70–71; guidelines, 132; ongoing communication with, 132–134. *See also specific organizations*

Grant-reviewing committee, 171–172

Grant-writing, 2; process, 170. *See also specific elements of grant-writing*

Graphs, 125

H

Hiring personnel, 87–88

Humane Society's Education Mini-Grant, 10

I

Illinois Learning Standards, 183

Impact, expanding, 55–57

Implementation plan, 130; chronological, 54–55, 63

In-cash matches, 90–91

Independent internal verification, 101–102

Indirect costs, 88–89

Informal learning tools, 184

ING Unsung Heroes Awards Program RFP, 60

In-kind matches, 91–92

Instructional unit, 173–181; grant, 182–185

Instructors, 53

Investing in Positive Academic Development. *See* IPAD

Invoice, 93

IPAD (Investing in Positive Academic Development), 58

J

Jerry McGuire, 2

K

Key word use, 7

L

Language: adjectives, 28–30; key word, 7; play on words, 58; slang, 25. *See also* Terminology

Large pot approach, 94

Learning: evaluation, 184; formal and informal tools, 184; statements, 182

Ledger: of deposit and expense, 95; example, 96; records verification and, 101

Ledger activity: answer worksheet, 159–160; worksheet, 151–152

Lenski Covey Foundation (LLCF) Library Grant Program, 11–12

Lesson reflections, 111–112

Let's Play land use grants, 76, 78

Letter of intent or letter of inquiry (LOI), 9

Likert survey template, 143

LLCF. *See* Lenski Covey Foundation

Local community foundation, 5

Logbook. *See* Ledger

LOI. *See* Letter of intent or letter of inquiry

Lyons, Katie, 182–185

M

Matching: grants, 77, 90; in-cash, 90–91; in-kind, 91–92

Measurable outcome, 47, 49, 59, 112, 118

Media release, 134

Mentoring sessions, 140

Money management, 93; double checking numbers, 96–97; financial reporting and, 95–96, 103; fiscal agent and, 94–95; reporting and, 102–104; security, 97–102; template, 96

N

Naming project, 57–58

Narrative, 134

Needs assessment, 122–123; Eat SMART, 173; in evaluation rubric, 171; identification and, 139; No More Desserts in the Desert, 178; From Tupac to Tennyson: A Spoken-Word Poetry Revolution, 182

Needs statement, 34, 37–38, 45–47, 52; anecdotal evidence in, 41–43; answer worksheet, 155–156; checklist, 141–142, 148, 155; data to include in, 40–41; under different prompt, 189; grant application without, 43–44; problem types in, 39–40; proficient example, 141–142; worksheet, 148

Next step, 131

No More Desserts in the Desert, 178–181

O

Objectives: goals *versus*, 48–50; as identified in planning template, 139–140; in RFP, 51; specificity in, 182. *See also* Outcome; Writing objectives

Offend no one, 27

One-time award grant, 3, 161

Online retailers, 86

Online search, 7

Outcome, 15, 55, 140, 172; Eat SMART, 176; expected, 28, 49; measurable, 47, 49, 59, 112, 118; No More Desserts in the Desert, 180; stated in subtitle, 58

P

Parent engagement, data collection, 120

Participants, 49

Partnerships, 128; extended classroom projects and, 132–133; multiyear programming with, 133

Passive writing style, 24

Pay day, 93

Philanthropy News Digest (*PND*), 7–8

Photos, 101

Physical controls, 100–101

Piton Foundation, 5

Plan, 67–68; assessment and evaluation, 112–115, 132; documentation, 191–192; implementation, 54–55, 63, 130; project or program template, 139–140

Planning Lifestyle Activities for Youth. *See* Project PLAY

PLANT (Preserving and Learning About Nature Together), 58

Play on words, 58

Plotline, 52

PND. See Philanthropy News Digest

Point of view, 22–24

Politically correct terminology, 27

Politically incorrect terminology, 21–22

Preserving and Learning About Nature Together. *See* PLANT

Prioritization, 31

Private foundations, 4–5

Private sales, 74–75

Problem, 37–38; identification, 139; types in needs statement, 39–40

Professionalism, 21–22

Proficiency, 141–142

Program officer, 9

Project or program description, 34, 51–52, 61–64; basics, 53–54; chronology, 54–55, 63; components, 140; Eat SMART, 174–175; evaluation of, 58; in evaluation rubric, 171; expanding project impact, 55–57; naming project, 57–58; No More Desserts in the Desert, 178–179; prompts, 59–60; teacher travel grant example, 186–189; From Tupac to Tennyson: A Spoken-Word Poetry Revolution, 182

Project or program planning template, 139–140

Project PLAY (Planning Lifestyle Activities for Youth), 57; prompt, 146

Proposal, 8–9; as conversational, 20–22; evaluation rubric, 13, 171–172; examples of complete, 173–181; rewriting, 144, 146; statistics to support, 108–110; strengthening, 183. *See also* Request for proposal

"Proposer eligibility" section, 11

Purchasing, 71–75

Q

Qualitative data, 113–115

Quantitative data, 113–115

Quarterly reporting, 102

R

Recommendations, 125

Records, 128; keeping, 101; verification and ledger, 101

Rejection letter, 128–130

Relationship building, 135–136

Relevant information, 108

Report, final, 194–196

Reporting: assessment findings, 122–125; best practices, 124–125; dissemination and, 104; end-of-year, 133; financial, 95–96, 103; material, 103; methods, 103–104; quarterly, 102; timeline, 102

Request for proposal (RFP), 1, 8, 59–60, 136–137; analyzing, 9–16; example, 13–15; finding, 17; goals and objectives in, 51; health awareness evaluation rubric, 171–172; major components of most, 33–34; problem implied in, 39. *See also specific RFPs; specific sections*

Research. *See* Data

Resource coordination, 68–69

Resource funding, 1; From Tupac to Tennyson: A Spoken-Word Poetry Revolution, 182–185

Responsibility establishment, 97–98

Results, 49

Review: panel, 27, 129; proposal evaluation rubric, 13, 171–172. *See also* Evaluation

Review guide: first period, 17, 161; second period, 35, 161–162; third period, 65, 162; fourth period, 92, 162–163; fifth period, 104; sixth period, 126, 163–164; seventh period, 137, 164

Revolving deadline grant, 3, 161

Rewriting, 144, 146

RFP. *See* Request for proposal

Rolling deadline grant, 2–3, 161

S

Sales tax, 86

School: benefits to, 190–191; community follow-up communication, 134; district initiative, 133; grants available for, 167–169; personnel, 69

Schoolwide information, data collection of, 118–119

Schoolwide program, 133

Security: documentation procedures for, 99–100; independent internal verification, 101–102; physical controls for, 100–101; responsibility establishment, 97–98; segregation of duties and, 98–99

Segregation of duties, 98–99

Shipping, 81, 86

Shopping, 73–75

"Show me the money," 2

Single classroom project or unit, 132

Slang, 25

Socioeconomic status, 27

Sources, 4–8

"Specific rules or policies" section, 10

Staff, 53

Stakeholders, 69–71; communication with, 130; follow-up, 134; involvement, 135; recommendations from, 125; relationship building with, 135–136. *See also specific categories*

Statement of need. *See* Needs statement

Statistics, 107; proposal supported by, 108–110. *See also* Assessment process; Data

Student activities, 175; key, 182; No More Desserts in the Desert, 179

Student benefits, 190

Student-first approach, 27

"Submission process" section, 12

Subtitles, 58

"Summary of funding organization" section, 9

Supervisor, 128

Supply purchasing, 71–72

Survey, 42; template, 143

T

Tagging, 101

Teacher, 37; benefits, 189–190; effectiveness framework, 117; English, 28; grants available for, 167–169; travel grant, 186–193

Teaching method, 15, 172; Eat SMART, 175–176; No More Desserts in the Desert, 179–180

Technology longevity, 56

Telephone, 7

Terminology, 8–9; politically correct, 27; politically incorrect, 21–22

Thank-you letter, 127–128; after award, 131; after rejection, 129–130

Theft, 100–101

Third-person writing style, 22–24

Time, 49, 53

Timeline: budget, 68; Eat SMART, 175; No More Desserts in the Desert, 179; reporting, 102; section, 11–12

Tools, 19–20; learning, 183–184

Transactions, 151, 159

Transparency, 125

Twitter, 8

U

UNITE, 5–6, 68, 75–77, 141. *See also* GET SCIENCE!

UNITE Classroom Grant, 3, 40, 137; RFP, 59–60

Updates, 132–134

V

Vendors, 73–74

Vision, 172; Eat SMART, 176–177; No More Desserts in the Desert, 180

Visuals, 125

W

Walmart Foundation, 5; Community Giving RFP, 60

Who, what, where, when, why, and how (five Ws and how) questions, 53

Windy City Youth, 76, 78–79

Word count, 31–33, 52; answer worksheet, 153–154; worksheet I, 144; worksheet II, 146

Worksheet: budget, 149; ledger activity, 151–152; needs statement, 148; word count I, 144–145; word count II, 146–147. *See also* Answer worksheet

Writing goals, 47–50

Writing objectives, 47; essential components, 48–50

Writing style: active, 24; composition, 20–31; consistency in, 30–31; conversational, 20–22; evidence based, 28–30; factual, 25–27; first person, 22–24; passive, 24; third person, 22–24

Y

You. *See* Author

Z

Zeist Foundation, 4, 12